The Five Wives of Maurice Pinder

Matt Charman's first play, *A Night at the Dogs*, won the Verity Bargate Award for new writers and was performed at the Soho Theatre in 2005. He is a recipient of the Peggy Ramsay Award, and is currently Pearson Writer in Residence at the National Theatre.

MATT CHARMAN

The Five Wives
of Maurice Pinder

faber and faber

First published in 2007
by Faber and Faber Limited
3 Queen Square, London WC1N 3AU

Typeset by Country Setting, Kingsdown, Kent CT14 8ES
Printed in the UK by CPI Bookmarque, Croydon, CR0 4TD

A CIP record for this book
is available from the British Library

978-0-571-23866-8

2 4 6 8 10 9 7 5 3 1

For Anwen

I'd like to thank Nick Hytner for popping me on a train to Manchester to meet the wonderful Sarah Frankcom. I'd also like to thank Jack Bradley, Elizabeth Freestone, James Westcott, Nina Steiger, Ti Green, Michael McCoy, Sebastian Bourne, Dinah Wood, Lucy Davis and everyone at the NT Studio. Thanks also to Anwen Hooson and the rest of my family for getting so excited.

The Five Wives of Maurice Pinder was first presented in the Cottesloe auditorium of the National Theatre, London, on 13 June 2007. The cast, in order of appearance, was as follows:

Fay Clare Holman
Vincent Adam Gillen
Esther Sorcha Cusack
Lydia Martina Laird
Maurice Larry Lamb
Rowena Carla Henry
Jason Steve John Shepherd
Irene Tessa Peake-Jones

Director Sarah Frankcom
Designer Ti Green
Lighting Designer Mick Hughes
Music Olly Fox
Sound Designer Rich Walsh

Characters

Maurice
early fifties

Esther
early fifties

Fay
early forties

Lydia
late thirties

Rowena
early twenties

Vincent
seventeen

Jason
very early thirties

Irene
mid-forties

Setting
A house in Lewisham, London

Act One: a week in summer
Act Two: a week in winter

THE FIVE WIVES OF MAURICE PINDER

The action takes place over three playing areas: the living room, the garden and a second-hand two-berth caravan parked in the garden. It's a family home on a budget, so everything is used and well worn. The garden is attractive but a little overgrown, with a damaged fence running along its back and down one side. A washing line is planted in the ground next to the caravan. A skeletal extension is being added to the rear of the house, but construction seems to have stalled. We can see the outline of the breeze blocks and the wooden baton of a planned window but that's all. There is no single style throughout this house – in fact there is a coming together of styles, of combined possessions and an accumulation of furniture.

Act One

SCENE ONE

Monday night. The house is dark and quiet.

Fay sits alone in the garden. Her head is back and her eyes are closed so she appears to be asleep. She has a half-drunk glass of wine and a packet of cigarettes on the table next to her. She looks stunning in the moonlight, almost like she's lying in state.

We hear a noise from the back of the garden. Fay doesn't stir. In the darkness we can make out a figure coming over the back fence but we can't yet see a face. With only a little effort, Vincent makes it up and over the fence and with a final vault lands with both feet in the garden. Fay doesn't move.

Vincent walks forward into the light and we see him properly for the first time. He looks at Fay and at the garden. He makes his way past her and towards the house. He is quite serious about not waking her or being heard at all. After he's taken a few steps Fay speaks suddenly without opening her eyes.

Fay Relax, he isn't home yet.

Beat. Vincent turns.

Vincent I am relaxed. I'm fine.

Vincent waits a moment before he slowly comes and sits down opposite Fay. He looks at her again and as she still has her eyes closed he quickly has a sip of her wine which he puts straight back.

We hear a cry from the baby monitor on the table. Fay reaches out towards the monitor, but picks up her wine glass instead. Vincent looks at her. She manages to take a sip, still without opening her eyes, a feat which he tries not to be impressed by.

There's another murmur from the monitor. Fay has another sip. Vincent looks at her harshly. He sighs.

I'll go then, shall I?

Fay Esther'll go.

Vincent You could go for a change.

Fay doesn't move, so Vincent stands. Just as he does so, we hear a woman's voice soothing the baby over the monitor. Vincent stops when he hears it and comes back to his seat. Fay hasn't moved.

When I have children of my own –

Fay (*with her eyes closed*) Normal boys your age don't think about that, Vincent. They think about sex, not kids.

Vincent Men can get broody too. (*Beat.*) When I have children of my own –

Fay (*with her eyes closed*) You're seventeen years old with a book of baby names under your bed. You know how I feel about that. You really ought to have pornography under there.

Vincent (*forcefully*) When I have children of my own . . . I'll be doing things differently to this . . . that's all.

Inside the almost dark house we see Esther slowly descend the stairs in a dressing gown. She ties her

*hair up and disappears into the kitchen, switching
on the light as she enters.*

*Back in the garden Fay reaches out and picks up
her packet of cigarettes. She still hasn't opened her
eyes but manages to take one and light it up.
Vincent shakes his head and slips off his shoes.*

Fay Have you made a short list . . . of baby names?
From your baby book. (*She opens her eyes suddenly
and looks at him.*) I know you have, it's written inside
the front cover.

Vincent I started making a list and I stopped myself.

Fay Good.

Vincent I realised I wouldn't want to force an identity
onto my child. We're going to wait until he's old
enough –

Fay Sorry, we?

Vincent My wife and I.

Fay Oh . . .

Fay takes a sip of wine.

Vincent We're going to wait until he's old enough . . .
and then we'll let him choose his own name.

*A spray of wine comes out of Fay's mouth as she
laughs and coughs at the same time.*

(*Concerned.*) . . . Mum?

*Fay is bent over now, still coughing and laughing.
Vincent stands up to help her.*

*Esther exits the kitchen with an empty washing
basket. She enters the garden and hurries to the
patio when she hears Fay coughing.*

5

Esther What's the matter?

Vincent Wine came out of her nose.

Esther kneels next to Fay and pats her back gently.

Esther Don't smoke *and* drink. Choose one at a time.

Fay (*recovering herself*) Did you know about this?

Esther Don't talk yet. (*She looks at Vincent's feet.*) Where are your shoes? It's dewy. Don't take wet feet to bed. Where have you been?

Vincent It's too hot to sleep. I've been walking around.

Esther stands and begins stripping the washing line of clothes. Pause.

Fay What will you call it till it's picked a name? (*Beat.*) You haven't thought about that, have you?

Vincent (*on the contrary, he is ready*) Reports suggest there's no need to name a child in the first two years.

Fay Reports? I thought you read books?

Vincent I read both. We'll talk to him face to face with eye-contact. Eye-contact does away with the need for names. Names are for sloppy parents with sloppy parenting skills.

Fay (*to Esther*) Did you hear that?

Esther (*without turning*) Names come in handy, Vincent.

Vincent I don't think so, not at the start of a child's life. They're restrictive. They tell a child what they're going to be. What you expect of them.

The baby cries again. Esther is poised. She stares at the monitor. The baby settles. Silence.

Esther Don't you like your brother's name?

Vincent doesn't answer.

Fay How will you get the baby's attention before it's picked its own name?

Vincent I've said – it's all about eye-contact.

Fay We couldn't have done that with you. You were boss-eyed until you were three.

Vincent I wasn't.

Fay Esther?

Esther A little bit boss-eyed.

Fay You'll end up whistling or snapping your fingers to get the baby to turn round. It's a horrible thing when a parent whistles at a child.

Vincent No whistling or stamping or shouting up the stairs to get a reaction. I won't do that. If I have a question for them I'll go upstairs, knock on his or her bedroom door and ask if I can come in.

Fay You'll ask a two-year-old permission to come in?

Vincent (*exasperated*) Why shouldn't a two-year-old be entitled to the same privacy as you or I?

This question hangs. Fay smokes. Vincent calms down. Esther continues taking the washing from the line. Pause.

Esther If we'd have left you alone when you were two, you'd have been dead within seconds.

Fay Of course he would.

Esther (*nostalgic*) You had a death wish. Jumping off the coffee table with things in your mouth. Like a

Japanese pilot. (*Beat.*) Never using a door if you could climb through a window or over a fence.

The baby cries again. Esther is poised.

Fay Wait . . .

The baby goes quiet. Esther picks up the monitor and cradles it.

Esther (*hurt*) What's wrong with the name Fergus?

Vincent It's a bully's name.

Esther No, it isn't.

Vincent It's the English version of the Gaelic, Fearghas. Derived from *fear*, which means 'man', and *ghas*, which means 'force' or 'strength', I think. Anyway, 'man of force' is sort of what it means.

Fay (*to Esther*) He's got a book of baby names under his pillow.

Vincent Under my bed.

Esther Your father liked the sound of Fergus. (*Beat. She looks at the monitor.*) And we never shouted up the stairs at you.

Vincent I know.

Esther That felt a little bit like a personal attack.

Vincent It isn't.

Esther Once or twice we called your name for ease, but we never bellowed.

Fay It isn't a personal attack, Esther. He's very grateful for the way we raised him, aren't you, Vincent?

Vincent (*dry*) Very.

The door of the caravan suddenly opens and Lydia climbs out, wearing a dressing gown.

Fay Sorry, Lid.

Esther Did we wake you?

Lydia (*shaking her head, a little crotchety*) No. Other idiots talking about baby names at the top of their voices sat outside a caravan made entirely of tin woke me.

Esther She's being sarcastic. (*To Lydia.*) They're not wearing shoes.

Lydia Neither am I.

Esther There's a dew.

Lydia (*to Vincent*) Stand up.

Lydia lays her hand on Vincent's shoulder and he jumps up willingly to give her his seat. She sits down and holds out her hand to Fay, who takes a long drag and plants the cigarette between Lydia's fingers.

Vincent I don't understand how you can smoke before bed.

Lydia (*taking a drag*) Don't let it worry you.

Vincent I mean you clean your teeth, you have a wash . . .

Fay You wash before you go to bed?

Vincent Don't you?

Fay Who washes?

Lydia Good boys wash. (*She passes the cigarette to Fay.*) Leave him alone.

Fay (*to Vincent*) Why do you do that?

Vincent This isn't about me, it's about smoking at night.

Fay You wash – what, your face? Doesn't that wake you up? I never taught you that.

Vincent I taught myself.

Esther Leave him, Fay.

Beat.

Fay Vincent was talking about the way we raised him.

Lydia Really?

Fay He's very grateful.

Lydia Pleasure.

Esther picks up her basket. It's full now.

Esther Fergus has been crying.

Lydia (*shaking her head*) We have to stop using that name. It isn't even definite yet.

Fay He's nine months old. What's wrong with it?

Vincent It's a bully's name.

Lydia Maurice is keen, but I'm working on him.

Esther He sounds a bit croupy.

Lydia (*concerned*) Really?

Esther Only a bit. I'll look in on him. (*Beat.*) Who's coming to bed?

Fay I am.

Fay takes a final drag and passes it back to Lydia. Esther looks at Vincent.

Vincent I'm waiting for Dad.

Lydia They'll be late.

Vincent I'll wait.

Fay Have a wash, stay alert.

Esther I'm going in. Lid, dry your feet, won't you?

Esther goes to move indoors.

Vincent Esther . . . (*He stands and takes something from his back pocket.*) Would you give him this?

Esther turns back and sees Vincent holding a letter in his hand.

Esther What is it?

Vincent (*shy*) It's from the university. It's nothing we didn't already know. It's just confirming my place . . . I'd like you to give it to him.

The women look at Vincent proudly. Lydia and Fay watch as Esther steps over and gives him a quick kiss.

Esther (*proud but sad*) You're all set, then.

She takes the letter, adds it to her basket and disappears inside. Vincent watches her go.

Lydia (*to Vincent*) You have no idea how much she'll miss you. (*Beat.*) Are you waiting up, Fay? Did you both stay up and wait for me? I can't remember.

Vincent I'd have been too young.

Lydia You weren't that young. It's only been three years. (*Beat. She thinks about this.*) Three years . . . You would tell me if I was turning into Esther, wouldn't you?

Fay You're not turning into Esther.

Vincent And it wouldn't matter if you were.

Lydia Yes, it would. She's acting like nothing's happening. She should be nervous.

Fay So should we.

Lydia That's why I'm worried I'm turning into her. We should be jealous or anxious, shouldn't we? She stays the same no matter what you throw at her.

Vincent That's a good thing.

Lydia No, it isn't.

Vincent Yeah, it is, it's called being constant. From a child's point of view it's comforting having something stable. She's the glue. Families need Esthers.

Lydia looks at him and frowns.

Fay He's been reading reports.

Lydia nods, takes a final drag of the cigarette and offers it to Fay, who declines. Lydia stubs it out.

Lydia Don't sit out here all night, Vincent.

Vincent Just until he comes.

Lydia (*she stands*) He could be hours yet. It's a long drive.

Fay What do you think she'll be like?

Lydia shrugs and smiles a little sadly.

Lydia She could be anything. Look at us, he obviously goes for variety.

Lydia climbs back into the caravan and shuts the door. Fay stands.

Fay (*to Vincent*) Night.

Vincent You haven't been a bad mother.

Fay (*surprised; beat*) I know.

Vincent Oh . . . I thought you might think you had, based on my comments just then.

Fay No.

Vincent Okay . . .

Fay heads for the house, enters and disappears upstairs. The house is still now. Vincent sits in the darkness of the garden for a moment. The front door opens. Maurice, a well-built, good-looking man in his fifties, enters carrying a suitcase. Rowena follows him inside. She's a very skinny, very pregnant girl in her early twenties, with a small cast on her arm. Maurice puts the suitcase down and looks at Rowena, who seems nervous.

Maurice All right, then?

Rowena (*shaky*) Yes.

Beat. Maurice smiles.

Maurice You'll be fine.

He calls up the stairs.

. . . Esther!

Rowena Don't.

Maurice Nobody's asleep, they're all too nosey.

After a moment Esther appears at the top of the stairs. She ties up her hair as she descends. She waits on the bottom step before smiling at Rowena

*and opening out her arms. Rowena steps forward
and hugs her awkwardly. Maurice seems happy.
Rowena steps back and picks up her bag. Esther
hands Maurice Vincent's letter, which he opens and
reads while Rowena moves for the stairs.*

I'll bring that. I'll be right up.

*Rowena puts her bag down and goes upstairs,
hesitantly. Maurice glances at the letter again and
then at Esther. He exits the lounge and comes out
into the garden. He walks straight over to Vincent
without saying a word and, full of pride, hugs his
son. He can't stop smiling. The lights fade.*

SCENE TWO

*Tuesday night. Early evening in the garden. Esther is
setting out the cutlery. The table is covered in a pure
white cloth. Lydia is picking up a few toys from the
garden. In her hand she has the monitor, which she
puts on the table.*

Lydia I can't smell anything.

Esther It's all in the fridge.

Lydia It's salad, then?

Esther Just in case.

Lydia In case of what?

Esther She's got limp hair. She may be vegan.

*Lydia looks up at Esther and watches her for a
moment. She seems concerned.*

14

Lydia Are you okay?

Esther smiles but continues to lay the cutlery. Lydia gives her a hand.

(*Beat.*) Who cooked?

Esther Vincent.

Lydia I don't eat on Vincent nights.

Esther Lay a place for yourself.

Lydia Okay, but I might not eat, I'll say that now.

Esther Lay a place for yourself.

Lydia Where's Fay?

Esther Lay a place for her as well. She'll be back.

Lydia looks at the table.

Lydia We're definitely going to need a bigger table soon.

Esther (*firmly*) No, we're not.

Lydia looks up at her again. Vincent enters carrying two kitchen chairs. Maurice follows, carrying a jug of squash and some glasses on a tray.

Lydia We're going to need a bigger table soon, Maurice.

Maurice We'll squash up.

Esther Of course we will.

Lydia Is she coming down? How is she?

Maurice A little bit intimidated.

Lydia Fair enough.

Vincent It's completely fair enough.

Vincent heads back indoors. Maurice puts down the tray and looks at Esther.

Esther (*quietly*) Fergus pulled himself up today. By the washing line. Just for a second.

Maurice (*smiling*) That's wonderful.

Esther nods and heads indoors. Maurice watches her go.

Lydia (*when she's gone*) Have you spoken to her today?

Maurice I phoned her from work.

Lydia Have you put your arms round her though? This part is hardest on Esther.

Maurice That's why I phoned her from work.

Lydia You're terrible on the phone, Maurice. Nobody ever knows where they stand with you after you've called them. She was like this when I came and it was the same with Fay, wasn't it? (*Beat.*) How young *is* she?

Maurice (*uneasy*) She's getting ready, she'll be down in a minute.

Vincent enters, carrying six large plates. Maurice changes the subject.

(*To Vincent.*) So where's your mother?

Vincent (*shrugging*) We're laying her a place.

Lydia I called but she didn't pick up.

Maurice (*tetchy*) Well, lay her a place.

Lydia It's being done. Relax . . .

*Lydia puts her arms round Maurice's neck and
kisses him softly on the cheek.*

. . . and go and put your arms round Esther.

Maurice (*sulking*) I'm fine on the phone.

He heads for the house and enters the lounge.

Lydia That's nerves.

Vincent He doesn't get nervous.

Lydia He does, and that's it written all over his face.

*Esther comes out of the kitchen with a salad bowl.
Maurice takes it from her. He smiles and carefully
puts his arm around her. They embrace and he
whispers something in her ear. She smiles warmly
and they head outside.*

  *Lydia moves the monitor over towards her and
sits down. Maurice pulls out a chair for Esther,
who sits and smiles up at him. Vincent stands and
gives the salad a toss proudly. He sits and then
remembers something. He takes the salt and pepper
grinders from his trouser pockets, one from each.*

What we're eating is salad-based, Vincent.

Vincent You can have salt on salad.

Lydia You don't have salt on salad.

Esther No salt for Maurice, it's bad for him.

Maurice Who made this?

Lydia Vincent.

Maurice We'll start the no salt tomorrow. Hand them
over.

Vincent passes the grinders over to Maurice. He sits. Pause. They all sit in silence.

Vincent Now what?

Lydia We wait.

Pause. They sit and wait. Inside the house we see Rowena slowly descend the stairs. She enters the living room and looks terrified. She stops, straightens what she's wearing and then, thinking better of it, quickly moves back up the first few stairs. She stops, changes her mind and decides to go with the outfit she's got on. She crosses the living room and emerges into the garden. Everyone looks up at her. Rowena stops dead. Maurice rises.

Maurice Okay?

Lydia You look lovely.

Rowena doesn't move.

Maurice Okay, then. Sit next to Lydia there.

Rowena walks to the spare seat next to Lydia. She holds the back of the chair with both hands.

Rowena Thank you for this.

Maurice nods. Rowena sits, then he sits.

Lydia We didn't know what you liked, so we decided on salad. Besides, it's Vincent's turn to cook and he's pretty bad.

Vincent Don't pre-judge, let her taste it first.

Lydia passes the salad bowl to Rowena. She puts the bowl down and clasps her hands in the prayer position. They all stop and look at her.

Maurice No.

Rowena looks up a little startled.

Rowena (*nervous*) Some people with big families are religious.

Maurice Not this one.

Rowena (*embarrassed*) Sorry.

Vincent (*softly*) Are you religious?

Maurice No, she isn't.

Vincent (*to Maurice, sternly*) If she is, she ought to be allowed to pray. (*To Rowena.*) We can pray if you want to.

Maurice She doesn't want to.

Rowena I'm fine, really.

Vincent (*to Maurice*) Maybe you should have told her you're not religious.

Maurice (*dry*) I should go round telling people that?

Rowena I'm sorry. (*Beat.*) It just occurred to me that you might be, with the tablecloth and . . . sorry.

Maurice (*smiling*) Don't worry, let's eat.

Rowena is embarrassed. She takes a few leaves of salad and passes the bowl on to Lydia, who keeps it circulating.

Lydia How did you sleep?

Rowena Fine, thank you.

Maurice That house is like an oven at the moment.

Rowena Whose is the caravan?

Lydia Mine.

Rowena Is that nice?

Lydia If you like being on a permanent camping trip.

Maurice It's only short term.

Rowena (*to Lydia*) Did I take your room?

Lydia No, I've been out here a little while. I like my own space.

Maurice The extension is for Lid.

Vincent When he finally gets round to finishing it.

Lydia There's no rush.

Maurice flicks a glance at Lydia. Vincent looks at Rowena.

Vincent How's your room? Is it to your liking?

Maurice You sound like a hotel manager.

Vincent I'm being polite.

Rowena It's very nice. (*Beat.*) Which one is your mum?

Her question surprises everyone. Vincent laughs a little. Lydia sits back.

Esther The children belong to all of us.

Lydia (*beat; under her breath*) Fay. She isn't here.

Maurice She should be. I'm sorry.

Esther You're too soft on her.

They eat. Maurice adds salt. Esther gives him a look, so he cuts back on it a little.

Lydia How was the journey?

Rowena Nice.

Lydia He didn't make you listen to his awful Spanish cassettes then?

Rowena Only for an hour or so.

Lydia Maurice!

Maurice She doesn't mind. She's supportive. The car's the only place I get to hear them.

Lydia That's because they're banned from the house. You must realise how dull it is for the passenger.

Vincent Really dull.

Rowena I don't mind, I think it's romantic.

Maurice I'm on Tape 2, Side A. Sickness and Emergency. 'I've cut myself, I've burned myself.' *Me ha picado una medusa.*

Vincent Meaning?

Maurice I've been stung by a jellyfish.

Vincent On Lewisham High Road? That's unlucky.

Maurice (*smiles; beat*) I spend the day with metal poles and men, and I'd be surprised if I used a hundred different words in an eight-hour stretch. But when I drive home . . . *¿Es de piel autentica?* 'Is this genuine leather?' It's useless and I'll never use it, but it keeps a door open up here.

Lydia Well, I'd like to kill whoever got you started on them.

Maurice Someone in the office lent them to me. Besides, you know what they say – it broadens the mind.

Vincent It's travel that broadens the mind, they don't say anything about GCSE Spanish.

Maurice laughs warmly. There is a comfortable pause. Rowena relaxes.

Rowena I'm trying to remember what Fay looks like. Maurice showed me a photograph of everybody.

Lydia Which one?

Maurice (*pointing to Vincent*) His birthday, last year.

Lydia So you knew what you'd let yourself in for?

Rowena Maurice told me about all of you . . . eventually.

Beat. They eat.

Esther Are you a vegan?

Rowena No.

Esther Are you anorexic? Your hair's in poor condition.

Rowena (*surprised*) No. I've . . . just got thin hair.

Everything falls a little flat. They eat. Rowena looks at Esther for a moment.

(*With strength.*) Are you married to Maurice?

Esther I was the first.

Rowena How long?

Esther Thirty-two years.

Rowena That's older than I am . . .

Esther There's a rota for basic jobs, so we don't need to go into that, but things like sleeping arrangements are a bit more involved.

Maurice Let's just eat for now.

Esther (*looking at Rowena*) You're very serious. He said you made him laugh.

Rowena You need to get to know me to find me funny.

An awkward pause.

Lydia So . . . Maurice mentioned you worked in a gallery.

Rowena A little museum. It also had paintings. I wore one of those waistcoats. Not security, but making sure nothing got vandalised, so almost like security but not trained. I sort of went mad standing around in that waistcoat hoping someone would vandalise something. Maurice used to come into the gallery. After a few visits I recognised him and started talking to him.

Maurice Walked straight up to me.

Esther He knows a lot about art.

Maurice I don't – I only know a tiny bit, but I love it.

Esther When he's away on business he always tries to get a place to stay near a gallery.

Maurice Just standing there. Calms me down.

Rowena In the place where I worked, there was this portrait that looked just like Maurice, but impressionist . . .

She looks at Maurice uncertainly.

Maurice That's right.

Rowena (*smiling*) Anyway, this portrait could have been a mirror . . . well, not a mirror but . . . it looked a lot like him and he never realised, and once he was standing in front of it and I came up next to him and said, 'What do you think?' and he said it was ugly.

Maurice Which it was.

Rowena He said that, but it wasn't. (*Pause.*) I bought a postcard of it from the gift shop. I've still got it. (*Beat.*) Sorry . . . that story didn't really go anywhere.

Maurice looks at her and smiles. They all eat.

Vincent What happened to your arm?

Maurice Vincent!

This hangs in the air for a moment.

Esther We used to go to galleries all the time. Before the children.

Lydia (*to Rowena*) Can you cook?

Rowena Yes.

Lydia Thank God.

Lydia smiles. Vincent takes this to heart.

Vincent You can't afford a single mistake in the kitchen, Rowena. I burnt something once and it's stayed with me ever since. Young men shouldn't be able to cook is the preconception. It's more fun if I can't, but I can, and I've got a pretty strong record of some reliable dishes, but I burnt something once so that's it for me now.

Lydia I'd love to be a fly on the wall in his first week at uni – watch him in the kitchen.

Vincent I'm in halls and they cook for you.

Lydia Just as well.

Maurice Vincent's going off soon. (*Beat.*) Tell her what you got in your A-levels then.

Vincent Dad . . .

Maurice What? (*Beat.*) I'll tell her they moved you up a year in a minute and really embarrass you. (*Beat.*) Lydia is a dietician. For old people. (*Beat.*) She also knows massage.

Lydia Maurice, this is excruciating.

Maurice I want Rowena to know all about you. I'm proud.

Lydia (*taking a deep breath*) I do Reiki. (*Beat.*) Do you know what that is?

Rowena I don't.

Vincent That's because it's a made-up word.

Lydia (*smiling*) Vincent's a non-believer.

Rowena (*genuine*) In what, sorry?

Vincent In bullshit.

Lydia In alternative healing. It's a safe method of spiritual healing and self-improvement.

Vincent As opposed to the many dangerous methods.

Lydia rolls her eyes and smiles.

Maurice And she writes too. She's published.

Lydia Hardly. (*Embarrassed.*) We had to pay to get a poem in a book they printed. Maurice paid for me to be in it.

Maurice She's in a book on a shelf in our lounge. I think that's as published as anything gets.

Esther (*beat*) Where's Fay? It's Tuesday.

Vincent We called, she didn't answer.

Lydia She's bad with days.

Vincent How can you be bad with days?

Lydia She's bad with days of the week and left and right. People have weaknesses.

Rowena Are you all married to Maurice?

Lydia In a way.

Esther (*going to stand*) I'll call Fay.

Lydia We called her.

Maurice It's okay, Esther. Sit down. They called her. Eat your food, it's all right.

Vincent (*beat*) How are you finding the salad, Rowena?

Maurice Again the hotel manager rears his head.

Rowena Tastes good.

Vincent (*touched*) Thank you.

The front door opens. The meal outside continues. Fay enters followed by Jason, who is smiling nervously.
  She shuts the door. She makes her way over to the sofa. He follows her. She sits, he sits. They look at each other. He reaches out and puts his hand on Fay's knee. She smiles and sits back. He smiles and looks around; suddenly his confidence slips.

Jason Nice. Open plan.

Fay Sorry?

Jason The room. It's very open plan. You've knocked down your supporting walls.

Fay (*looking around; beat*) Yes, I have.

Jason It's very brave.

Jason has one final glance around before looking back to Fay. He feels a little silly with his hand still on her knee. She senses this and works a little harder.

Fay (*seductively*) I like your tie.

Jason Thank you very much. (*Beat.*) I like the way you smell.

They smile at each other. He looks around again and takes his hand away.

. . . It looks like a family home. (*Beat.*) Is it? . . . How do you find those new wheeled bins that the council have delivered?

Fay (*impatient*) Adequate.

Jason I just mean you can get a special dispensation for a large family, you know. A bigger bin, I think. Two bins even. (*Beat.*) Is it a large family? (*Beat.*) Is it your family?

Fay You were more fun half an hour ago.

Jason Well, I wasn't expecting a house. Well, I was expecting a house, but not such a . . . whole . . . house. Like a home. A family home. (*Beat.*) I will be fun again, bear with me. (*Beat.*) A drink would help.

Fay I find not thinking too much about the sex usually helps.

Jason Right . . . So that's still on the cards, then?

Fay Did I bring home the wrong man?

Jason No.

Fay (*beat*) Sit.

He sits back and tries to relax. Pause. He is awkward and doesn't know where to put his hands. She eyes him and smiles.

Jason I know this area quite well. These streets. The architecture. (*Beat.*) Look, I'm not going to lie to you –

Fay Don't lie to me.

Jason I'm not going to lie to you. (*Beat.*) Having said that, I want to make clear that I may have exaggerated my experience . . .

Fay You've got some?

Jason Some, but I think I probably laid it on a bit thick in the bar. (*Beat.*) This is . . . (*He looks around*) new to me.

She notices he is squinting a bit.

(*Beat. He looks around.*) I'm just getting my place the way I want it. It's a long-term project. (*Beat.*) I saw a chair. I liked it and I bought it, chrome and leather . . . it's uncomfortable but it looks good. Now I need another to sit in for comfort, because I can't sit in the other one for long.

Jason starts squinting again and shielding his eyes.

Fay (*frustrated*) Why don't I just sit over there?

Jason Would you mind? . . . Every time your head moves I'm staring right at the bulb. It's like a little sun, you know.

She moves and resents it.

Fay (*settling*) Here?

Jason That's better . . . Thank you.

An awkward pause. Jason refocuses on Fay and realises she's older than she first appeared in the dark bar.

Fay Hobbies?

Jason Yes. (*Beat.*) Why?

Fay (*shrugs*) I don't know. I'm trying to lighten the mood a little bit. I'm clutching at straws.

Jason (*beat*) I rock climb.

Fay Outdoors?

Jason Not yet. You have to train for a long time indoors, it's actually very dangerous. People see the rope holding you up and think it's not dangerous but it's actually very dangerous. (*Beat.*) I've got all the gear.

Fay Okay. Just calm down and lose yourself in the conversation. Let's get the old Jason back.

Jason (*sits upright and breathes out*) Films, I like.

Fay Everyone does.

Jason I read as well.

Fay (*smiling*) Do you?

Jason (*beat*) What?

Fay People say they read, but do you actually? I don't.

Jason I do.

Fay (*beat*) Carry on.

Jason I'd like a family. (*Beat.*) A couple of kids, a wife.

Fay It's not a hobby though, is it?

Jason No.

Fay Stick to hobbies for now.

Jason Okay, sport. I try and stay fit. I like team events but also individual . . . shit. (*Beat.*) I just clicked straight into interview mode. It's because you're a little bit older, I think.

Fay eyeballs him.

. . . Sorry (*Scared he's blown it.*) It's the sex thing – it's actually quite off-putting, when it's offered on a plate.

She looks at him.

Not on a plate, but when it's offered up . . . like that. When the work is done. Fuck. Forget it. Look, let's go back to the bar.

Fay (*ready to stand*) No.

Jason Let's go straight back now. Forget the wheelie-bin segment.

Fay I can't, I'm babysitting tonight.

Jason (*hurt*) What about us?

Fay I expected things to move faster.

Jason We met forty-five minutes ago.

Fay You're married.

Jason (*beat; self-conscious*) No, I'm not.

Fay Yes, you are.

Jason (*beat*) No . . . I'm not.

Fay It's no problem. It makes it easier. You've taken your ring off, right? You keep going to play with it but it isn't there. It's fine. It's better. I thought the bachelor-pad story was very sweet.

Jason That's not a story, that's true. We don't live together yet.

Jason looks at the space on his finger before plunging his hand in his pocket and pulling out a ring which he slips on.

Jason It's an engagement ring.

Fay Men don't wear engagement rings.

Jason I do. Debbie wanted everyone to know I'm –

He looks up at Fay.

. . . unavailable.

Fay That worked well.

Outside, Vincent picks up the jug and heads for the house.

Jason Let's go back to the bar.

Fay No.

Jason (*angry*) Why?

Fay It might have clicked. The right thing might have been said. It wasn't. You have to allow for that – it's fine.

Jason (*nods*) You're very harsh.

Fay So?

Jason Is that an older-woman quality?

Fay You should go.

Jason I paid for the taxi.

Fay Is that likely to swing it for you at this point, do you think?

Vincent enters with an empty jug in his hand.

Vincent Your phone's switched off. (*Beat.*) Who's this?

Fay Jason.

Vincent (*beat*) It's Tuesday night.

Fay (*confused*) Really?

Vincent Everyone's outside. We've been phoning you.

Fay (*beat; genuinely trying to work it out*) It doesn't feel like a Tuesday, it feels like a Thursday.

Vincent Well, it's Tuesday.

Jason It *is* Tuesday.

Fay Right. (*Beat.*) Right, well, everyone's outside so . . .

Jason So?

Fay Family night. Tuesday night. Every Tuesday. Family meal tonight, confirmed by you as Tuesday.

Fay throws him his jacket.

Jason (*stands and points at the jug*) What's that?

Vincent A jug.

Fay We're a family and it's summer. We eat outside and we serve squash in a jug. Bye, Jason.

Jason Who's this?

Fay is embarrassed.

Fay My son.

Jason (*beat; smiles angrily*) That's a bit fucked up, isn't it? (*Beat; speaking loud and slow to Vincent.*) I met your mum in a bar forty-five minutes ago.

Fay (*to Vincent*) Don't talk to him.

Jason (*to Vincent*) We were talking. She said your place or mine, I said mine. Then I remembered they're changing all the windows in my building this week, so she said her place. How old are you?

Vincent Seventeen.

Jason (*to Fay*) Don't you think it's a little bit warped?

Fay Go outside, Vincent.

Jason Vincent, don't you think?

Vincent exits into the kitchen.

I'm honestly . . . a little bit sickened. Is his father here?

Fay It's a Tuesday. It's a family meal – everyone's here.

Fay opens the front door.

Jason (*flustered*) It doesn't bother me that you're older.

Fay Thanks.

Jason But you shouldn't promise sex.

Fay I'll remember that.

She shuts the door on him. She turns. Maurice is standing in the doorway to the garden.

Maurice Vincent cooked. (*Beat.*) Rowena's here.

Fay I know. (*Beat.*) I'll change.

Maurice Where have you been?

Fay I'm sorry I'm late.

Maurice Where have you been?

Fay Shall I change? I smell of cigarettes.

Maurice There's a new member of the family outside. A place was set for you. (*Beat.*) Who was he?

Fay (*she looks at him*) I'm sorry I'm late. Let me shower and . . . I'll be right out.

Maurice Was he married?

Vincent steps into the kitchen doorway with a full jug of squash. He goes unnoticed by Fay and Maurice.

Fay (*sharply*) Does it matter?

Maurice If this is going to continue to work out . . .

Fay I know.

Maurice Then don't bring them back here, this is our home.

Fay (*with strength, testing him*) But me going back with them is all right, is it? Just for clarity?

Fay spots Vincent and goes quiet. Awkwardly, Vincent carries the very full jug through the lounge. He heads outside. Maurice waits till he's gone.

Maurice I don't stop you. You do what you have to do, just don't bring them back here. It hurts Vincent and it hurts me. (*Beat.*) Are you drunk?

Fay A little bit.

Maurice nods and looks at her sternly. Fay slowly steps out of her high heels towards him. They are standing close together now and facing one another. Neither one of them moves for a moment. She leans into him.

(*Flirty.*) Do we have to go straight out?

Maurice (*playful, smiling*) Yes.

Fay (*disappointed*) What's she like?

Maurice She fits in.

Fay Poor girl.

Back in the garden, Vincent is trying to eat.

Lydia Was he attractive?

Vincent I don't know.

Lydia You must know if he was attractive or not?

Vincent He was the same sex as me – I'm not equipped to judge.

Fay and Maurice enter the garden. Everyone goes silent. They approach the table and Maurice takes a seat. Vincent doesn't look up.

Maurice Rowena, this is Fay.

Rowena Hi.

Vincent (*beat; quietly*) You reek of cigarettes.

Fay Salad looks dry.

Fay sits. Vincent puts down a little jug next to her.

Vincent I don't put the vinaigrette on. I put it in a separate jug. Not everyone likes vinaigrette.

Fay Not everyone likes your vinaigrette. (*Beat. To Rowena.*) So what do you think?

Rowena Of what?

Fay Of us.

Rowena (*watching her step*) It's too early to say . . .

Fay First impressions, then.

Maurice Fay!

Lydia Eat some food, Fay.

Fay grudgingly takes the bowl and picks up a leaf, which she chews on. They eat.

Esther (*to Rowena*) We all work. You'll have to.

Maurice We do, we all work.

Rowena What do you do, Esther?

Maurice (*covering*) She's in charge at home here and we all do our own thing during the day. We all contribute.

Rowena What do you do, Fay?

Fay I sell magazine subscriptions over the phone.

Rowena (*smiles*) Really?

Fay Why not?

Maurice She's very good at it.

Fay I'm very bored with it. (*Beat.*) You can take over. I'll be your supervisor, if you like.

Maurice (*happy*) You could show Rowena what to do.

Fay I could try. It's rather a skill, selling people crap they don't want. (*Beat.*) Lid, tell her what you do.

Lydia She knows.

Fay (*dry*) We're a hive of industry. A beehive run entirely on salad.

Vincent Piss off. At least I know what day of the week it is.

Esther (*strong*) Vincent!

The company is surprised by Esther's reaction. Fay picks up another salad leaf.

Fay (*to Rowena*) What happened to your arm?

Vincent Don't ask her that.

Fay (*ignoring him*) Roweena?

Vincent (*correcting her*) Rowena.

Fay (*beat; kindly*) What happened to your arm?

Rowena My ex-boyfriend. (*She holds up her fingers.*) He broke these.

Vincent At the same time as he did that? (*He gestures to the cast.*)

Maurice Different times. (*Visibly upset.*) She had trouble for weeks. Every time I saw her, something else was broken. (*He gives up on his food.*)

Esther He takes everything to heart.

Maurice (*quietly*) Now everyone's here . . . I want to make a toast. Please.

Everyone slowly raises their glasses.

We welcome Rowena.

All Rowena.

Maurice I get . . . a lot of pleasure out of small things.
Seeing you all sat here. (*Self-conscious but heartfelt.*)
Your faces . . . eating at the same time around one
table, it's simple but it makes me happy. (*Beat.*) I'm
ordinary in every other respect but this family. I never
knew what that phrase meant, the sum of their parts.

Vincent (*quietly, but uncritical*) More than the sum of
their parts.

Maurice Well, that's what we are, an awful lot more.
(*Beat.*) The most important thing in the world is family.

*They all drink. Maurice sits. They pick up their
cutlery and begin to eat together. The lights fade.*

SCENE THREE

*Wednesday night. Maurice enters the caravan and
shuts the door behind him. Lydia is sitting on the bed.
She smiles. She and Maurice have made an effort for
each other.*

Maurice Your hair looks good. (*He touches his shirt.*)
Ironed by my own fair hand.

Lydia I'm impressed.

Maurice (*holding out something for her*) Here.

*She looks at what he's holding and then pats the
space next to her. He sits.*

For you . . .

She takes it, a little surprised. He smiles as she unwraps it. It's a small silver box.

Lydia That is beautiful, Maurice.

Maurice You like it?

Lydia I love it. It's very delicate. It's a pillbox, isn't it?

Maurice But you can keep jewellery in it. It's got a hinged lid and inside is lined – blue felt. This building site we're on, this job – it's opposite an antiques market. It only runs on a Wednesday.

Beat.

Lydia (*carefully*) Next time you should get something for Esther.

Maurice (*taking this on board*) Maybe I will. But that's for you. (*Beat.*) You like it, then?

Lydia It's perfect. (*She kisses him.*) Take your shirt off.

Maurice stands and takes his shirt off. He drapes it over a cupboard door and sits again with Lydia kneeling behind him. She begins to massage him and it has an instant effect. Maurice smiles and closes his eyes.

Can you feel that?

Lydia moves up to his neck. He knows what to do and drops his head down. She continues to work on him as she speaks.

I don't like Fergus as a name.

He is caught a little off guard. She goes on massaging him.

Maurice We can change it.

Lydia I said we'd live with it and see what I thought of it and on reflection I hate it. We can both decide on a new one. We ought to both be happy with it.

Maurice Of course we should.

Lydia Okay, let's change the name.

Maurice Okay.

Pause. She massages him in silence.

Lydia I need to go away.

Maurice (*flatly*) No.

Lydia stops massaging him and takes her hands back. He looks up.

Lydia You know I need to. Nothing's changed –

Maurice Of course it has.

Lydia shakes her head.

Of course it has with the baby now, things have definitely changed.

Lydia I haven't. Other people go travelling with a baby.

Maurice Families don't.

Lydia I wouldn't be travelling as a family.

Maurice This comes up every few months and then it goes away again.

Lydia No, it doesn't.

Maurice You can't travel with him on your own.

Lydia Yes, I can. I've always moved around. I always have.

Maurice You haven't been here long.

Lydia Three years.

Maurice That's nothing.

Lydia It is . . . for me . . . and I've been happy. Very happy, and I wanted to have Fergus and I wanted to stay here and look at myself hard and now I need to go away again. Maurice? I don't know how else to talk to you about this. I've said it every single way. You don't want to listen.

Maurice No, I don't, not tonight.

Lydia It's our night – if not tonight, when?

Maurice shakes his head.

I see Rowena and I think, that was me. It was. That was just like me, the way she was last night. Unsure and grateful . . . That isn't me any more.

Maurice You're bored.

Lydia I'm restless.

Maurice Same thing.

Lydia No, it isn't. I haven't put down roots here.

Maurice We've had a baby.

Lydia I live in a caravan. I don't live in the house.

Maurice The extension's for you, your own space. (*Apologetic.*) I've been distracted, I know that. I'll work harder on it.

Lydia (*firm*) Don't build it for me. I don't want it. (*Beat.*) I made it clear I would go away again. Maurice, you heard me say that.

Maurice is shaken by this. She softens.

We would never have got together unless I was like this. I'm grateful we did and we've had a beautiful son, but all the time I'm here I'm suffocating.

Maurice (*beat*) Esther needs the baby.

Lydia Esther needs help. She's depressed and you should take more care of her. (*Beat.*) I've been travelling since I was sixteen.

Maurice You drifted. No need to drift any more.

Inside, Rowena and Fay sit opposite one another in silence. Fay is smoking and staring at Rowena, waiting for her to say something.

Fay Again.

Rowena 'May I speak to Mr Bucknor, please?'

Fay (*beat*) 'Speaking.'

Rowena takes a breath and looks down at the piece of paper on her lap.

Rowena 'Hello, Mr Bucknor, my name is Rowena.'

Fay 'Do we know each other?'

Rowena 'No.'

Fay 'Then who are you and why on earth are you calling?'

Rowena 'I'm calling in relation –'

Fay 'Relation?'

Rowena 'Regarding –'

Fay 'I'm sorry, is this a sales call?' (*Beat. She smokes.*) 'Because it sounds just like a sales call . . .' Script!

Rowena looks back at her script. She turns the page and finds her place.

Rowena 'No, it is not a sales call – it's more a friendly call, really, to tell you about a special offer that might interest you.'

Fay 'I am interested. A special offer for what?'

Rowena 'A gardening magazine. A horticultural publication.'

Fay 'Is it free?'

Rowena (*she hesitates*) 'No, but it's –'

Fay 'I was in the bath. I have a bad hip. Why do you people always call me this time of night? What is wrong with you people?' (*Beat.*) I just hung up.

Rowena I can't do this.

Fay Yes, you can. (*Beat. Leaning forward.*) Look, if they sound phlegmy and old then they're probably bad old and the wrong demographic.

Rowena Bad old?

Fay (*she draws out another cigarette*) Don't waste your time. They only want someone to talk to. One sale a day is all you need. Brutality and telesales go hand in hand. Let's try again.

Rowena No.

Fay (*lights up her cigarette and takes a drag*) Look, just be fun, flirt, be suggestive. It works. With men and women. (*Beat.*) 'Mr Bucknor? Fay Pinder calling. Congratulations, Mr Bucknor, this is the golden hour. Are you sitting comfortably? I have something special to offer you and in about five seconds you'll be able to tell me if you want it or not.'

Rowena (*prudish*) I couldn't do that. (*Beat.*) One a day?

Fay Name, address, credit card details. The subscription company does the rest. (*She stands.*) Esther doesn't like me smoking indoors.

Rowena You have a dim view of men.

Fay I have a view. It's my view. (*Beat.*) You're entitled to your own.

Rowena Do you go out very much?

Fay (*smiles*) Is that a euphemism?

Rowena I don't know.

Fay (*beat*) Flexibility is good.

Rowena Not for everyone.

Fay No, not for everyone.

Rowena Esther seems . . .

Fay Esther loves Maurice more than all of us put together and she loves the children. It's worth it for her because of them.

Rowena But doesn't she – ?

Fay I don't have much patience. If something works I don't see the point in poring over it. I see him when I want. An evening a week and on family nights. I have my own space, which I've never had anywhere else. I love the girls – it's not like being a mistress.

Rowena No?

Fay No. I wouldn't let him use me. I'm not a secret he's keeping from other people. Do you think Lydia would let any man use her? (*Beat.*) I know his weaknesses. He knows mine. Look, he's not about to change. No one particularly wants him to. If it works for you, then stay. If it's not for you, then go.

Rowena Aren't you worried about when you get really old and I'm not so old?

Fay If you're number four, what makes you think there won't be a number five?

> *Fay leaves the lounge and enters the garden. She lights up a cigarette.*
> *Rowena picks up the phone-book and flicks through it. Vincent comes halfway downstairs and waits for a moment. He watches Rowena dial a number from the book. She hesitates and, hearing a voice on the other end, she hangs up.*
> *Vincent comes quietly down the last few stairs and into the room.*

Vincent Old?

Rowena (*a little surprised*) Who?

Vincent Were they phlegmy and old by any chance? Are you practising Fay's method of dealing with old people?

Rowena No, I'm not.

Vincent (*he sits*) Good, because it's a little bit fascist, I think.

Rowena Why don't you call her Mum?

Vincent Fay? Esther doesn't like it. I do sometimes.

Rowena throws the book to one side and looks despondent.

Rowena I don't think I can do this.

Vincent Fay hates it too, but she's brilliant at it as well as being too lazy to do anything else. Plus it gives her plenty of free time.

Rowena Doesn't Maurice mind?

Vincent What?

Rowena (*coy*) What she does with her afternoons.

Vincent Meeting men in wine bars you mean? (*Beat.*) Of course he minds, but he doesn't have any choice. It's part of the arrangement.

Rowena What about Lydia?

Vincent She isn't a predator like Fay.

Rowena You're talking about your own mother.

Vincent When I was six I sat in the passenger seat of our car with a coat thrown over me while she did it with a guy on the back seat. (*Beat; he smiles.*) I think that's funny. She loves it. She's very sexual. I've grown up with it. It's sent me completely the other way, I think.

Rowena You don't like sex?

Vincent (*embarrassed and showing his age*) Well . . . there are other things to be interested in right now . . . I mean, obviously I like it . . . I'm going to York because it's good for sex, apparently . . . and Humanities.

Pause.

What do you see in my dad?

Rowena He's calm.

Vincent Honestly?

Rowena Why not?

Vincent Is that attractive?

Rowena Yes. (*Thinking.*) I asked him to take me away from Ben and he didn't even blink. (*She touches her cast.*) He said it was like a sanctuary here. I didn't know what he meant.

Vincent (*beat*) I want certain aspects of his personality for myself. I want to hang on to certain bits and throw the rest out. I've spent weeks trying to laugh like him. Have you noticed his laugh?

Rowena smiles.

Right, you have. An amazing, proper man's laugh. I love his laugh. I've practised it.

Rowena Show me.

Vincent No.

Rowena Go on.

Vincent No, I haven't got it yet. It's an amazing laugh though, and I really want to steal it. And the way he chews food and talks at the same time but doesn't look like a slob – in fact he looks like an actor eating and talking.

Rowena What else?

Vincent I can't think . . . not much more. Not this. (*Beat.*) Not this set-up here.

Rowena You don't want a big family?

Vincent Of my own I do, not borrowed.

Rowena Is this legal, what we're doing?

Vincent shrugs and looks down at his feet.

Vincent Nobody's signed your cast.

He comes over, takes her pen and sits next to her.

(*Disappointed.*) . . . Maurice has.

Vincent thinks for a moment, then speaks as he draws a pattern on the cast.

Do you want to marry him?

Rowena He hasn't asked me.

Vincent He'll ask. Would you want to?

Rowena It would be a bit sudden.

Vincent (*smiles*) He'll make it sound like the most natural thing in the world. We'll have the ceremony right here. I'll cook. (*Beat.*) I've done that upside down so you can see it.

There is a knock at the door. He hands her pen back and stands.

Tell Maurice you hate telesales and that you'll find something else. He won't mind. Having a kid always shuts him up.

Rowena Don't say that.

Vincent It's true.

Vincent moves across and opens the front door. Jason is standing outside holding a bunch of flowers. Vincent is momentarily caught off guard. Pause.

Jason They're for Fay.

Vincent reaches to take the flowers.

I'd like to . . . give them to her, please. To apologise.

Vincent steps to one side. Jason enters and nods at Rowena. Vincent shuts the door.

Rowena She's in the garden.

Vincent points. Jason makes a move for the garden.

Vincent (*beat*) My dad's here.

Jason I know.

Vincent nods. Jason exits the lounge. Out in the garden Fay is still smoking. There is a half-shell paddling pool that Fergus has been playing in that day. Fay steps over to it and pours out the water onto the grass. She picks up a few toys while she continues to smoke. Jason steps outside. He is momentarily distracted by the extension. He looks closely at the brickwork before looking up and watching Fay for a moment. She turns and sees him staring.

There's still a hose-pipe ban in force.

Fay I'm sorry?

Jason I hope you didn't fill that with a hose-pipe. (*Beat.*) I'm joking.

Fay looks unimpressed as he walks towards her and lays the flowers down.

Fay You put those flowers down like I was in hospital. Who let you in?

Jason Vincent. Is that his girlfriend? (*Beat; looking at the flowers.*) These have been on the back seat of the car so they're a bit . . .

Fay (*holding a child's toy*) Don't worry, this one isn't mine.

Jason Of course not.

Fay Why, because of my advancing years?

We hear raised voices from the caravan and a little movement inside. Jason turns and looks up, but because Fay has acted as if she hadn't heard anything he does the same. Pause.

Jason . . . Nice garden. Big.

Fay Don't start making observations again.

Jason Okay. (*Beat.*) He's in there, is he?

Fay What do you want?

Jason (*beat*) It's a nice street. I drive past it on my way to work. It isn't the quickest route but . . . it always looks like a nice street, trees coming out the pavement. (*Beat.*) I want to meet him.

Fay looks surprised.

Maurice Pinder. Scaffolder. Owns his own scaffolding business, in fact. (*Beat.*) Spooky, isn't it? I work for the council, we've got a database. I can't access it myself, but a friend of mine can . . . it's a council tax database. There isn't much information there, don't worry.

Fay (*beat*) What is this?

Jason points at a chair. Fay doesn't respond but he sits anyway.

Jason I need to ask you . . . what you had in mind last night? For the two of us, I mean? (*He leans back.*)

Fay Aren't you embarrassed by conversations like these?

Jason I never have conversations like these. I've never done anything like that before.

Fay We didn't do anything.

Jason I know . . . but I mean . . . the idea of bringing someone back like that . . . when you're older and married and . . . it's not something I've been party to before.

He leans forward. She watches him.

I've never met anyone like you. (*Beat.*) From your point of view, what makes a person, you know, go out and do that? Look for that sort of thing . . . look for me?

Fay I wasn't looking for you.

Jason I think you were, in a way. (*Beat.*) I don't do things, anything . . . to rock the boat. Ordinarily. My own boat, I mean. My life is fine. I sit at home –

Fay In your leather and chrome chair?

Jason I sit at home and I don't rock the boat. I don't go after things, armed with flowers, and . . . I like you.

Fay You're saying the same thing on a sort of loop.

Jason I wanted to meet him. (*Beat.*) You came looking for me.

Fay I didn't.

Jason If you came looking for me, you must be unhappy with him.

Fay Maybe I'm greedy.

Jason You wouldn't need to be if you were with the right man.

Fay (*laughs; beat*) What about Debs?

Jason (*strong*) Her name is Debbie.

Fay Has she found the right man? What does it say about you and her? The fact you came looking for me?

He looks at Fay. She smiles back at him, surprisingly gently.

(*Softly.*) When's the wedding?

Jason (*quietly*) Saturday.

Fay This Saturday?

Fay smiles again, and can't help laughing a little.

Jason I shouldn't be here.

Fay No, you really shouldn't.

Jason I shouldn't be thinking about you either.

Fay Then stop.

Jason I can't. (*Beat.*) I needed to see you again. I'm not married yet and –

Fay laughs again.

(*Ruffled.*) It's an important distinction. When I marry her . . . that'll be it. (*Angry.*) Look, you can laugh, but you're the one in a singles bar looking for someone who isn't your husband. Looking for someone like me.

Back in the caravan. Lydia is watching as Maurice sits in silence.

Maurice You're being very selfish.

Lydia (*flaring up*) Of course I am. That's the beauty of the situation. Do you really think we stick around here because you're this incredible specimen of a man who makes speeches and builds extensions and knows three things about art? Fay wants her life the way *she* wants it, Esther wants a family she would never have had otherwise, and I wanted a baby and I wanted to bring him up around people who would love him and now I want to take my baby and go. (*Beat. She calms down.*) This will always be somewhere we can come back to. (*Beat.*) I love you, but this isn't what I need now.

Maurice I need all of you.

Lydia You don't need me. You can't say that you do.

Maurice This doesn't work without you, like it wouldn't work if any of us went. In time we'll need Rowena, we'll depend on her. Because we're a family. That's what happens . . .

Lydia We're not actually a family, Maurice . . . and this was never going to last for ever. All of us living like this . . .

Maurice (*standing*) I need some air.

The caravan door flies open and Maurice steps out with his shirt still in his hand. He's followed out by Lydia. He turns to walk back up the garden but lays eyes on Jason. He stops and goes quiet. Pause. On impulse Jason stands and offers his hand to be shaken. Maurice looks at him blankly. He waits a moment before he looks at Fay, and then passes Jason on his way into the house. Fay looks at Jason, then follows Maurice in. Jason seems surprised and half-expects her to come back. Pause.

Jason (*raising his voice*) Fay? (*He seems confused.*) Fay!

Lydia looks at him. He looks back at her.

. . . Sorry.

Lydia (*walks towards him*) Are you the one from last night?

Jason (*distracted*) What?

Lydia You're shouting. (*Beat.*) What's the matter?

Jason (*looking to where Fay disappeared*) She walked away. (*Hopeful.*) She might have gone to get me a drink.

Lydia She hasn't.

Jason That was Maurice, wasn't it? (*Beat. He sits and looks at Lydia for the first time.*) You don't look alike. Like sisters. (*Beat. It occurs to him.*) You're not sisters, are you? (*Beat.*) Do you live in that? (*He looks at the caravan.*)

Lydia She probably isn't coming back out.

Jason (*beat*) Were you in there with him? (*Beat.*) Can you tell me what's going on here?

Lydia seems to look at Jason for the first time. She takes in his whole body.

Lydia You've got an interesting energy.

Jason I'm sorry?

Lydia You're very fired up, aren't you?

Jason I was talking to Fay, we weren't finished. (*Beat.*) Why are there so many people around?

Lydia There aren't that many.

Jason Is it Fay's baby, can I ask you that?

Lydia He's my baby.

Jason What were you doing in there? (*Beat.*) What's he building here?

Lydia Did you come to see Fay?

Jason Yes.

Lydia Fay isn't here.

Jason I know.

Lydia That sort of makes you an intruder.

Jason looks at her. He picks up the flowers.

You can leave those.

He lays the flowers back down and walks halfway up the garden toward the house before he stops and turns back to Lydia.

Blackout.

SCENE FOUR

Thursday night. Esther quietly descends the stairs in a dressing gown with a cotton slip on underneath. She moves over to the CD player. She puts a CD in and retreats to the far side of the room with the remote control in her hand. Maurice emerges from the kitchen, wiping his hands on a drying-up cloth. He looks up and spots Esther. He smiles. Esther smiles back and points the remote at the CD player. Music starts up, soft and seductive but in truth a little embarrassing.

Maurice (*softly*) Come here . . .

Esther steps towards him. Maurice touches her cheek and they kiss. She draws her hand across his face and down his neck. She undoes one of his buttons and stumbles on the second. He helps her. She steps away and walks over to a cabinet beneath the CD player. She takes out a Christmas bottle of Scotch. She pours a glass. He watches her.

Could I have a pinch of lemonade? (*Beat.*) Sorry, it gives me heartburn neat.

Esther digs deeper into the sideboard cupboard and finds a bottle of lemonade. She pours it into the glass as Maurice steps over to turn out the corner lamp.

If we went out this weekend, just you and me, where would we go?

Esther (*pleased*) I don't know.

Maurice (*soft*) Where would you like to go?

Esther (*beat*) I don't know.

Maurice Ice-skating? Something stupid?

Esther Last time we went ice-skating it was 1982. You fell down and got water on the knee.

Maurice Something else, then. (*Beat.*) Anywhere you like, we'll go.

Esther (*she smiles*) Are you coming up?

She goes to move with the glass in her hand.

Maurice I need to go away – with Lid.

Esther (*stops and looks at him*) A holiday? (*Beat.*) Just the two of you?

Maurice Fergus as well. Just a break, just the three of us.

They look at one another. Maurice doesn't know how she's taken this.

I'm just trying to hold on to this . . .

Esther (*beat*) I'm going up now.

Maurice Yeah . . .

Esther moves for the stairs. Maurice watches her disappear out of sight and then turns off the music. He looks upstairs again, then heads out to the garden. He sees Vincent sitting reading at the table but nonetheless moves for Lydia's caravan. He knocks on it. No answer, so he knocks again.

Vincent She's gone out.

Maurice knocks again.

(*Raising his voice.*) She's gone out. There's a note.

Maurice (*looking*) Where?

Vincent stands up and goes over to the caravan. He peels off the note and gives it to Maurice.

It's too dark. I can't read it.

Vincent (*reading*) 'Back later – Lid.'

Vincent gives the note to his father and returns to the table.

Maurice Where's she gone?

Vincent I don't know.

Maurice We need to talk.

Vincent You and I?

Maurice Lydia and I.

Vincent I thought it was Esther's night.

Maurice It is.

Maurice steps away with the note still in his hand. He looks at Vincent.

You'll strain your eyes in this light.

Vincent Esther already said that.

Maurice Well, she's right. What are you studying? Exams are over.

Vincent It's preparatory reading. The university sends you a list. (*He holds up the book.*)

Maurice (*looking at the cover*) Degas. I don't like him.

Vincent (*quietly*) He speaks very highly of you.

Maurice stands restlessly with the note still in his hand. Vincent reads.

Vincent Good day at work?

Maurice (*distracted*) Long. We're working on a . . .

He looks back at the note again and drifts off for a moment.

Vincent (*looking up*) Dad?

Maurice . . . It's a block of flats. Quite modern.

Vincent (*nods; beat*) I heard the music.

Maurice It's Esther's CD, she loves it.

Vincent I think she thinks you like it.

Maurice takes a seat. He picks up a different book and flicks through it half-heartedly.

Maurice Cézanne could paint though, couldn't he? Where's the one I like?

Vincent She'll be waiting.

Maurice I'm just going up.

Vincent takes the book off him and flicks to a certain page. He hands it back. Maurice smiles. Vincent watches him.

Vincent I talked to Rowena.

Maurice Good. Are people making her feel welcome?

Vincent We like her.

Maurice flicks through the book. Vincent seizes the moment.

Do we really need another baby here, Dad?

Maurice (*beat; taking this in*) I thought you liked babies.

Vincent I do.

Maurice Fay says you go on about children all the time –

Vincent I don't.

Maurice – which I'm pleased about. Do you want a big family?

59

Vincent (*pushing through*) Here, though. Do we need another baby here?

Maurice She's in trouble.

Vincent So are a lot of people.

Maurice I wish I could help them all. Vincent, her fingers were broken by a man who couldn't face up to his own responsibilities. When people stop doing things like that then I'll stop taking people in under my roof.

Vincent (*correcting him*) Women.

Maurice Women under my roof.

Vincent It's not that I . . . I know what you do and a part of me is proud.

Maurice A big part, I hope.

Vincent It is . . .

Maurice See things from my side, Vincent.

Vincent We always do, Dad. (*Picking up his book.*) Please go upstairs. Esther's waiting. It's her night and she looks forward to it. You owe her, her night. You owe her a lot more.

Maurice (*smiling*) Are you giving me advice now? (*Beat.*) 'Two things people will always need are food and scaffolding.' My father said that to me. 'Go into either food or scaffolding and you'll always have a job.' (*Beat.*) When have I ever said that to you?

Vincent (*reluctant*) You haven't.

Maurice No. I've said go into fine art or be a writer or weave hedges or be a scientist because I want all things for you, and I'm not afraid for you either because these women have opened me up. They've rewritten me. When I met your mother she changed me. She was spirited; she gave herself over to anything. That's infectious and life-changing. I shouldn't be like this after the way I was brought up. I shouldn't be able to live like this, want this. But I do.

Vincent Please go up.

Maurice stands and looks at his son. Something catches his eye in Vincent's book.

Maurice You see . . . (*Passing it to Vincent.*) See that doodle? (*Beat.*) Even your doodles are good.

Vincent (*looking at the doodle*) Do you know what it is?

Maurice Don't dismiss your old dad, Vinnie; we're happy more than we're not. I've got some of the answers, haven't I?

He walks away, then stops. He comes back a few steps.

I'm gonna ask Rowena to marry me.

Vincent looks angrily at his father.

(*Beat.*) The grass is wet, don't be much longer.

Vincent stands and quickly gathers up his things. He goes inside. As he enters the lounge a key turns in the lock. Rowena walks in, followed by Lydia, pushing a pram. Rowena sees Vincent disappear up the stairs. After a moment Maurice enters from outside.

Maurice (*to Lydia*) I just came out looking for you.

Lydia His cough's come back. We went for a walk. Shouldn't you be upstairs?

Maurice I'm going.

Rowena shuts the door and looks downcast. Maurice sees this.

How was your day?

Rowena Fine. (*Beat.*) Lydia took me up to the shops but they're shit. They all only sell phonecards and incense. (*Beat. She looks at him intensely.*) Have you told her yet?

Maurice frowns and nods to Lydia.

She knows.

Maurice What do you think, Lid?

Lydia It's good. I'm pleased. What does Esther say?

Maurice I'm just going up.

Rowena You'll tell her now?

Maurice nods, but he hesitates.

Go on, then. She'll be waiting for you. (*Beat.*) I'm not going to listen.

Maurice There won't be any noise.

Rowena There's always noise.

Maurice After thirty years of marriage there isn't any noise, believe me.

Rowena What's Fay like in bed? I bet Fay's a good lover.

Maurice (*beat*) See you in the morning.

Maurice stays standing on the spot. He looks at Rowena. Esther arrives at the top of the stairs.

Esther Maurice?

Maurice looks up and smiles at Esther, who smiles back nervously.

Rowena That's a lovely nightie.

Esther Thank you. (*Beat. She holds out her hand.*) Maurice?

Maurice climbs the stairs to her and they move out of sight.
   Pause. Lydia watches Rowena.

Lydia It's Esther's night, there's nothing to hear.

Rowena doesn't move. Lydia comes down to the sofa. She kneels at the opposite end to Rowena and pats the space in front of her.

Come here.

Rowena swivels her body and lays down. Lydia puts a cushion under Rowena's knees and cradles her head. Rowena closes her eyes.

Rowena Doesn't it bother you?

Lydia (*beat*) You'll get used to sharing him.

Rowena On your night . . . does he stay?

Lydia My mattress is foam and three inches thick. He stays the nights his back can take it, otherwise he goes back to Esther. (*Beat.*) Can you feel that in your left ear?

Rowena Yeah.

Lydia There's a flow of energy to your left, just a little one.

Lydia lowers Rowena's head and lays her hands on her chest.

Rowena (*nervous; venturing*) What's . . . what's the sex like?

Lydia Good. Sometimes we just cuddle and talk or I give him a massage. Sometimes we make love.

Rowena Is it ever boring?

Lydia Who doesn't get sick of having sex with each other? Sometimes they want it and you don't and your mind is elsewhere. You get bored and drift off. I always end up thinking about how cassette tapes work. (*Beat.*) That isn't any different for a couple than it is for us four sharing him. He never forces you to do anything. He's very gentle. (*Beat.*) I don't suppose you two have –

Rowena Not yet. (*She touches her stomach.*)

Lydia Well, when you do, you take control. (*Beat.*) Can you feel this?

Rowena It's hot. He broke a rib. Ben did. Here. (*She touches her body to show Lydia.*)

Lydia (*beat*) Makes sense. The body rushes to fix the parts that need it.

Rowena (*beat*) I think I might want him all to myself.

Lydia Maurice? You might.

Rowena Then what?

Lydia Kill us one by one.

Rowena (*she smiles*) Would you come and live like this again?

Lydia No.

Lydia's answer surprises Rowena. They hear voices upstairs. Rowena opens her eyes and stares up at the ceiling. They both listen for a moment, then hear a noise, something stifled and awkward. Not a shout, but almost.

Esther emerges a moment later on the stairs. Her hair hangs loose around her shoulders. She looks unpredictable and dangerous. Vincent arrives at the top of the stairs in boxers and a T-shirt. He comes down a few steps.

Vincent What's the matter?

Rowena sits up. Maurice arrives next to Vincent with his shirt undone.

Maurice Esther?

Esther walks over to Rowena.

Esther (*to Lydia*) She's staying.

Lydia Of course she is.

Maurice It's your night. Come back to bed, Esther.

Esther stares down at Rowena. She is unsure whether the older woman wants to hit her or hug her. She is scared. Esther throws her arms around a confused Rowena. She grips her in a suffocating embrace.

Esther If I could have had children . . . do you really think any of you would be here? If you're staying, you ought to know we share everything. It all blurs. You and that baby will, too. You ought to know that from me because nobody else will say it.

Vincent (*softly*) Esther?

Vincent comes down a few steps. Esther looks up at him. She calms down, stands and walks towards him. He hugs her. Maurice remains standing on the landing. Rowena looks uncomfortable.

Blackout.

SCENE FIVE

Friday night. Esther and Lydia are playing cards in the caravan. Fay is standing just outside the door, smoking. She's dressed for the evening and looks incredible.

Maurice is working on the extension. He looks up at Fay from across the garden. She smokes and looks back at him. She taps her watch lightly and he nods.

Rowena steps out of the kitchen into the lounge. She has the phone pressed to her ear and a glass of orange juice in her hand.

Rowena (*into the handset*) In terms of quality, this magazine is superior to what you can buy over the counter. It's the heavy paper that makes all the difference.

There is a knock at the door. She moves across to it.

It means they use more colour than normal. The flowers look real . . .

She opens the door. Jason looks back at her. After a moment he steps inside. He has a rucksack on his

66

*back and is dressed casually for a night out, with a
shirt and jeans and a chunky diver's watch. He
steps into the middle of the room and looks around
it while Rowena sells.*

. . . vibrant. The word magazine doesn't do it justice.
(*Covering the handset and calling.*) Maurice! (*She gets
no reply.*) Okay, let me just say . . . no, no, let *me* say –
It's a horticultural publication. Gardening but also
crafts. It's bought to be collected, really. It should
come with a binder. (*Beat.*) No, it doesn't come with
a binder.

> *Rowena is aware of Jason watching her. She turns
> her back to him.*

'Get quick and easy tips for determining the grade of
the shade in your garden and even discover strategies
for letting in more light.' Do you like roses? (*She
reads*). 'See how Rosarians group roses by their origin,
history and characteristics, and get tips on the forms
and habits of ten rose types.' No? Okay. (*Beat.
Disappointed.*) Okay . . . thank you. (*She hangs up.*)

Jason (*beat*) Is Fay in?

Rowena (*looks at him suspiciously*) They're going
out. It's her night.

> *Jason has a seat. They both stare at one another.*

Jason How are you finding it? Living here . . .?

> *Rowena looks at him suspiciously and doesn't
> answer. Maurice enters the house. He stares at
> Jason for a moment.*

Maurice Did you call me?

Maurice looks at Rowena. He nods to her. She steps outside and immediately heads down the garden. Rowena walks quickly down to the caravan.

Fay What is it?

Rowena He's back.

Lydia Again? Three times in one week –

Fay goes to make a move. Esther stops her.

Esther Fay, don't.

Fay I'm not going in. I just wanted to see. (*Beat.*) Maybe I should go in . . .

Esther You should stay here.

Fay reluctantly stubs out her cigarette and steps inside the caravan. There's a flash of excitement on her face. Rowena steps in after her and sits down.

Fay What did he say?

Rowena Nothing – what do you think he wants?

Lydia Isn't it obvious?

Beat. The women look at Fay. Esther deals the cards. In the lounge, Maurice looks proudly at Vincent's painting hanging on the wall. Jason is sitting on the sofa, also looking at it.

Maurice My son painted it. Aged eleven. He has a real eye I think for . . . His mother's brains, but a little bit of my eye for art, I hope. He used to rearrange the fruit in the bowl. Said he was making it more appetising. Used that word aged seven. Smart like his mum.

Jason opens his rucksack and takes out a notepad. Maurice points at it.

Jason It's for my notes. (*Beat.*) I have access to a database at the council. You're on the electoral roll, so is your wife Lydia Pinder.

Maurice It's Friday night.

Jason I know.

Maurice I'm taking Fay out.

Jason She calls you her husband.

Maurice Yes, she does.

Jason But you're not married to Fay?

Maurice I was.

Jason But you're not now?

Maurice (*beat*) Fay's sorry for leading you on.

Jason (*beat; hurt, then defensive*) And she asked you to say that, did she? Do you read the Riot Act to all her boyfriends?

Maurice And that's you, is it? (*Beat; more friendly.*) She's an incredible woman. She talks to anyone – I mean she can make conversation with anyone.

Jason I know.

Maurice She has a way with people straight off. Intimate, close. Some people don't understand that, they get confused. She's sorry for leading you on but . . . you're embarrassing her by coming over here.

Pause. Jason sits still and looks back to the painting.

Jason What is it?

Maurice Oxygen bubbles. Three of them. Fay, Vincent and me.

Jason You're very cool about all this. I mean, you are her husband . . . aren't you? She calls you that, doesn't she? But it says here you're married to Lydia. (*Beat.*) Do you understand my confusion? (*Beat.*) You're not married to both of them, are you? And the young girl? And the baby? Is he yours?

Maurice looks at him. A long pause follows, which Jason takes as a proof of guilt.

This is illegal, then – how you live?

Maurice No.

Jason Tell me why not.

Maurice (*beat*) I get divorced.

Jason You marry, then you get divorced? So you're not married to Fay any more?

Maurice We're still married because of the words we've said to one another. Paperwork doesn't change that. It's the words that count.

Jason At the registry office?

Maurice The important words are exchanged at home. The registry office is just the paperwork part.

Jason So you're divorced, you just choose not to recognise it? (*Beat.*) Society –

Maurice Tell me about society.

Jason Society won't tolerate this. It finds it abhorrent. Living this way.

Maurice Have you asked society?

Jason I am society. I pay for things. I vote for things and I wear things out and I'm telling you this situation only exists in a nasty little vacuum until society knows it exists, and now it knows. (*Beat.*) I want to know what happens here. I want to see in your kitchen.

Maurice (*confused*) What?

Jason I have to know what goes on upstairs.

Maurice looks at him. Jason looks down, embarrassed.

Maurice How many good marriages do you know?

Beat. No answer.

What do you do . . . for the council?

Jason I'm a planning officer, Mr Pinder.

We hear a restless, slightly croupy cough from the monitor in the caravan. Esther stirs but doesn't move. Out in the garden Vincent jumps over the fence and lands on both feet. He has his earphones in, so he's speaking loudly.

Vincent (*heading for the house*) I'm back as promised. God forbid I should actually go out on a Friday night and have a bit of fun. (*Beat; dry.*) Overrated if you ask me, drinking and fondling people.

Vincent passes through the extension and enters the lounge. He stops dead when he sees Jason.

Jason Hello, Vincent.

Vincent Dad?

Maurice (*beat*) It's all right, go outside. Carry on if you like, I've made a start.

Jason Please don't touch anything out there, not yet.

Maurice You know what you're doing, don't you? Just change your jeans first. I'll be in trouble with Esther if you get those dirty. (*Beat.*) Go on.

Vincent looks back at Jason and then quickly goes upstairs. Jason lays his folder on the coffee table.

Jason Are you religious?

Maurice No.

Jason You're not a Mormon?

Maurice No.

Jason I saw a television programme about them.

Maurice I didn't see that.

Jason They do this. (*Beat.*) I checked the database and it had Lydia's name on the electoral roll, but Fay had said –

Maurice I'm not a Mormon, I'm not religious.

Jason But you are polygamous?

Maurice You seem keen to give this a name.

Jason Well, what would you call it?

Maurice My family.

Jason (*beat; with authority*) I believe you've carried out unauthorised work to this house. (*Beat.*) There are no records appertaining to any applications. (*Beat.*) You don't have planning permission for that extension, Mr Pinder.

Maurice I know.

Jason Why didn't you apply for it?

Maurice I knew I wouldn't get it.

Jason (*beat*) What are you building?

Maurice I have to change. I'm taking Fay out.

Jason You already said that.

Maurice Then why are you still here?

Jason (*beat*) Tell me about what you say to them. To get them to stay. To live like this. If you divorce them, why don't they walk away?

Maurice Are you jealous of me?

Jason Yes, I am, I like Fay. (*Beat.*) If you divorce them –

Maurice We're still married because of the words we've said to one another. You're married for time and eternity. It's our own ceremony.

Jason You can't do that.

Maurice It isn't illegal.

Jason You can't just make up your own ceremony.

Maurice Well, how do you think they normally start? (*Beat.*) The vows we make . . . they're just between us and because of that they mean more. It is a bond. God isn't involved.

Jason You're a pervert. (*Beat.*) This is a perverted way to live. How old is the new girl?

Maurice Her name is Rowena. You should go.

Jason Is she next? She's very young. You're middle-aged. That's disgusting. (*Beat.*) She's got a cast on her arm.

Maurice She's been mistreated.

Jason And she's pregnant. These women are unbalanced.

Maurice Really?

Jason Unhappy and unbalanced, and I think you trick them . . . talk them into things when they're at their lowest ebb. Defenceless. Is that true?

Maurice stays silent.

You didn't answer my question . . .

Maurice It's a bedroom.

Jason (*raising his voice*) Another bedroom? Then what? Another one after that? Where does this end?

Maurice You'll wake my son.

Jason I'm gonna need to see it . . . your extension. (*Beat.*) Was it your idea to fill this house with women?

Maurice These women, all of these women are independent and strong, I can't tell them anything. They do as they like. Fay went out and met you, I didn't stop her.

Jason It's because she's unhappy.

Maurice It's because of who she is. You don't know her.

Jason I think I do. You can't be a husband to all these women. She wouldn't act like this if you were a proper man.

Maurice (*a flash of anger*) And that's you, is it? Picking up women in bars and hiding your ring finger? Fay told me all about you. I don't lie to them like you lie to her . . . Debbie, isn't it?

Jason (*caught out, but determined*) Here's how it works. As an enforcement officer I can gain entry to your home either via Section B of the Police and Criminal Evidence Act or a subsection of the Town and Country Planning Act that I can never remember. Take your pick.

Jason takes some ID from his pocket. Maurice stands and takes it. He reads it and hands it back. Jason goes to move.

Maurice Wait . . .

Maurice looks ill. He stands slowly and steps over to the door to lead Jason outside. Once out in the garden Jason looks at the extension and makes some notes. He takes a camera from his rucksack and takes a few photographs. Maurice looks around the garden. He calls out.

Fay?

The caravan door opens. Jason turns. Fay steps out followed by Lydia (holding the monitor), Rowena and finally Esther. Jason looks at Fay for a moment before turning back and taking another photograph.

Jason What will you be rendering it in?

Maurice Brick.

Jason Fletton brick? (*Beat.*) Fletton brick is a pressed brick.

Maurice I know what it is –

Jason The rest of the house looks like it's rendered in handmade local stock brick. Brickettes two and a half inches deep.

Maurice It'll be done in local brick.

Jason (*making a note*) Have you notified your neighbour? Have they got a basement? A lot of properties round here have. Your foundations may undermine their basement. How deep are they?

Maurice A metre.

Jason That's fine. And you've taken precautions against radon?

Maurice Yes.

Jason (*doubtful*) Have you?

Maurice Yes.

Rowena What's radon?

Jason A gas. (*To Maurice.*) Would you mind telling me what precautions you've taken?

Maurice (*frustrated*) Cavity trays. And I've connected the damp-proof membrane with the cavity tray and I've vented the underfloor void.

Jason (*a little put out*) Fine. (*He makes a note.*) I'll need the architect and the builder's name?

Maurice That's my name.

Jason I would advise you to cease work immediately. Failure to do so will make you liable to a fine of £2,000 with a further fine of £50 per day for every day the contravention exists.

Fay What are you doing?

Jason (*ignoring her*) I'll put all this in writing. You'll have to make a retrospective application.

Maurice We're not hurting anyone.

Jason Yes, you are.

Maurice The neighbours don't mind.

Jason (*a flash of anger*) I mind. Who do you think you are? This is a conservation area.

Maurice I'm building this for my family.

Jason Well, I'm protecting it for everyone else's. (*Beat.*) The rules apply to us all. You think they don't, but they do. You can't just spread yourself out in the world and make up ceremonies and live this way. A family is a man and a woman and a child or two – or more – but it's a man and a woman and it certainly isn't this.

Jason looks down the garden at Fay. He hesitates.

I've sent her a letter, Fay. To tell her about you.

Fay (*gently*) You should go.

Jason (*to Fay*) I've put it in writing to her. You brought me back here for a reason. I really believe that. You chose me.

Maurice You could have been anyone. Tell him, Fay.

Jason No, I don't think so . . .

Jason looks at her; she looks back at him strangely.

Don't you want to hear it? What I wrote to her.

Fay No.

Jason It's about you. (*Unable to hold back.*) 'Dear Debbie.' (*Beat.*) 'This is the hardest thing I have ever had to write and I want you to know that because it's certainly true.'

77

Fay What are you doing?

Jason It's what I wrote. (*With real difficulty.*) 'I have met someone that I never intended to meet. I went to a bar after work with a colleague, with Peter, from accounts, on Tuesday and I met this person and everything changed for me.'

Maurice laughs a little but Jason won't be thrown off. A long beat.

'I can split my head in half and in one half I can live with you and I can see everything we had planned and I can understand how that could go on for ever and we could be happy. But in the other half my head is full of Fay and there's no end to that in sight and not in a good way.' (*Beat.*) 'I love you, Debbie, and I love her –'

Maurice suddenly laughs again, longer and harder this time. It only fires Jason up more.

'– and they are different kinds of love and one has beaten the other and won and it isn't you and that's the only way I can explain it.'

Fay looks at him. Jason struggles to regain his composure. He looks around at all the women and finally back to Fay. He seems cleansed to have said this and a little emotional. She looks at him, but we can't read her reaction.

Fay I'm sorry . . . if I led you on, but . . .

Jason looks devastated. Fay looks down.

Jason (*beat*) You're in a lot of trouble, Mr Pinder. You think there's nothing I can do about this situation?

Maurice We're not breaking the law.

Jason That is . . . (*He points at the extension.*) You have no idea what's within my remit. What I could make them do.

Jason looks at Fay, hoping she might look up at him.

(*Desperate.*) You choose this, then, Fay?

Beat. He gets no answer. He glances at the other faces watching him.

I hope I've fucked up your evening.

He exits the garden, enters the house and slams the front door shut behind him. Everything is silent for a moment. Maurice looks at Fay.

Fay You had no right to tell him he couldn't see me any more.

Maurice That's what you go looking for in the afternoons, is it, Fay? (*Beat.*) Come inside, please, it's our night.

Fay No.

We hear a whimper on the baby monitor. Esther goes to make a move but Fay holds her back.

(*Vulnerable.*) Stay . . . please.

Esther is torn. She stays where she is. We hear Vincent's voice soothing his brother over the monitor. Then silence. After a moment Vincent heads downstairs and towards the garden.

Maurice You invited him into our home. That's why we have rules, Fay.

Fay You have rules.

Maurice We have rules. (*He moves down the garden towards her.*) You know I could be like that if you wanted. A bully like that. Fay?

Vincent Dad? What's the matter?

Maurice Come inside, please . . . He won't ruin our night. He wanted to, but he won't . . .

Fay You had no right. I see who I like.

Maurice Fay, come inside please.

Fay stays still. We hear the baby again on the monitor.

Lydia . . . Our son needs changing. (*Stronger.*) Lydia, Fergus needs –

Lydia That isn't his name.

Maurice (*without control*) THAT'S HIS NAME.

No one moves. Everyone is shocked by his ferocity.

Vincent Dad?

Lydia I'll go, Maurice. (*Beat.*) If this is the way it's going to be then I will take the baby and go, I'm serious.

Esther No . . .

Lydia I will – we're not here for rules, you know that.

Maurice (*slowly and with growing emotion*) I will not have this family broken up by a man with a fucking database. (*Beat.*) You won't go out looking for men like that any more, Fay. You won't need anyone else from now on. (*Beat.*) Do you understand me?

Fay doesn't respond.

Rowena (*quiet but urging*) Maurice.

Maurice (*to Lydia*) And you – you'll be in that extension by Christmas and that's an end to it. No more talk of going away. This is your home. (*Beat.*) Vincent, see to your brother.

Vincent doesn't move. The baby keeps crying.

Vincent, I said see to your brother. Come inside, Fay . . . it's your night.

Vincent shoots a nervous glance at Fay, who stays rooted to the spot, as all the women do. Maurice walks across to her and stands just inches away. He is emotional but resolute. He is turning a corner and he knows it. Fay stares back at him.

It's your night, Fay . . . It's your night.

Blackout.

Act Two

SCENE ONE

*Winter, three months later. Monday night. We hear
a noise at the back fence. A rucksack slides down it,
landing in a heap on the grass. A moment later a body
scales the fence and drops down into the garden. It's
Vincent. A term at university has subtly changed him.
From his dress and his demeanour we notice now that
he has one foot firmly in manhood. He glances round
the garden. The extension has grown, but is nowhere
near being complete. It's decorated with brightly
coloured Christmas lights. The garden is unchanged,
although it's now in winter mode with an outdoor
gas-heater on the patio and all but one of the chairs
upended on the table. Vincent steps over to the patio
and puts his bag down on Fay's chair (the only one
out and facing the garden). He immediately spots
something, and reaches down, pulling out an empty
wine bottle from behind a chair leg. He looks at it,
slightly embarrassed, and puts it back. He steps down
from the patio and across to the caravan. He hesitates
a moment and then knocks lightly on the door. After
a moment the door opens and Rowena steps forward
into the light. Her baby bump is gone now. They look
at one another.*

Vincent Hello, Mum.

*She gives him a look and he smiles back at her. He
nods at what she's wearing.*

Never thought I'd see you in –

Rowena (*whispered*) Shhh! You'll wake her.

Rowena turns back and checks on the baby.

Vincent Sorry. (*Beat; dropping his voice.*) Can I have a look?

Rowena (*whispered*) Quickly, don't let the heat out.

Rowena steps to one side, allowing Vincent to lean into the caravan for a moment. He pulls his head back out and smiles.

Vincent (*whispered*) She's a serious baby. I like serious babies. (*Beat.*) It's Monday night, I thought Maurice would be –

Rowena His back can't take this mattress for long.

Vincent Why isn't she in the house? Fergus always slept in the house. Isn't it too cold?

Rowena (*defensive*) Don't you start. Esther keeps on at me day and night. She's convinced she must be freezing to death out here.

Vincent Isn't she?

Rowena (*firm*) I know how to look after her. We're fine. I'm keeping her with me. (*Beat; changing her tone.*) I thought it was tomorrow you were –

Vincent I got an earlier train. (*Beat.*) So . . . Zoë, then?

Rowena What do you think of it?

Vincent I like it.

Rowena (*pleased*) So do I.

Vincent It's Greek, it means life.

An awkward pause.

. . . I'm sorry I couldn't get down earlier to see her.

Rowena Don't worry. (*Beat.*) What were you gonna say before?

Vincent Oh, nothing. Something sarcastic about your nightie.

Rowena Don't, I'm getting old, aren't I? (*Beat.*) How's it been, then? The course and everything? Your first term? Michaelmas . . . isn't that what they call it?

Vincent (*smiles and nods*) It's okay.

Rowena No tan?

Vincent No . . .

Rowena I thought you might have a tan. (*Beat.*) York's coastal, isn't it?

Vincent Not really.

Rowena You look older, anyway.

Vincent You should see me in a nightie, I look ancient.

Rowena (*beat*) We missed you, everyone has. Especially Fay. I think she expected you back at half-term.

Vincent (*defensive*) It's called reading week, and I needed to work. There's a lot to do. It's a long way for just a few days, you know. (*Beat.*) How is she?

Rowena Not great. (*Beat.*) Esther's been so excited.

Vincent That's nice.

Rowena Yeah, it is. Means she might even leave Zoë alone for a bit now you're back.

Vincent Don't say that.

Rowena Maurice is like a dog with two tails. He's been racing around. He put the lights up this weekend. It's all for you.

Vincent How's married life treating you, then?

Rowena Just the same as unmarried life. (*Beat.*) Go on, he'll be waiting.

Vincent (*reluctant*) It's all right, no one's expecting me till tomorrow.

Rowena He can sense you're here, though, I bet.

Vincent turns and looks at the house. He seems unwilling to move. He steps away, then turns back with a strange expression.

Vincent (*anxious*) What's Irene like, then?

Rowena (*beat*) Organised. (*Beat.*) Welcome home, Vincent.

Rowena smiles and shuts the caravan door. Vincent steps over to the patio and picks up his bag. He also reaches down and picks up the bottle. He walks through the lit extension and enters the dark house, dropping his bag off his shoulder and proceeding through to the kitchen to drop the empty wine bottle into the bin. He steps back into the lounge, walks over to the corner lamp and switches it on. He looks around the room and takes it in: first the unlit Christmas tree in the corner, then his painting, which still occupies pride of place on the wall. On the stairs behind him Maurice appears, wearing a dressing gown and peering into the darkness. He watches Vincent for a moment before he speaks.

Maurice I'm friendly with the artist, you know.

*Vincent turns and looks up at him. Maurice goes
to speak but Vincent puts his finger to his lips and
silences him. Maurice nods and comes down the
last few stairs. They hug one another and smile.
Maurice playfully pulls at his son's jacket.*

(*Whispered.*) What's this, then? Been spending our
student loan on fashion have we?

Vincent (*dry; looking at his dad's dressing gown*)
Thank God I don't get my dress sense from you.

Maurice I thought we had intruders. I grabbed the
first thing I could find. I don't fight anyone naked,
I don't care who they are.

*Maurice smiles and moves over to a chair. Vincent
sinks into the sofa.*

Vincent (*beat*) I like the lights.

Maurice They look better when they're on.

Vincent They are on.

Maurice Are they? (*He looks in that direction.*) They
shouldn't be, they're on a timer.

Vincent Well they're still on.

Maurice (*beat*) I'll take a look at that tomorrow.

*Maurice straightens his dressing gown. Vincent
watches him. An awkward pause. Vincent looks
back at the painting.*

Vincent That's no good, you know.

Maurice Of course it is.

Vincent No – when you don't look at it every day and
you suddenly see it again, you realise how bad it is.

Maurice It's perfect.

Vincent It's not, Maurice.

Maurice (*playful*) You're doing a degree in art history, what do you know? (*Beat.*) It's you, me and your mother. Each other's oxygen.

Vincent Are you always so deep this time of the night?

Maurice Always. (*Beat. He smiles.*) Your mother's missed you. We all have.

Vincent (*defensive*) There hasn't been a lot of opportunity to call, this first term. It's been so busy, you know.

Maurice (*nods, unconvinced*) How is it?

Vincent (*beat*) It's okay.

Maurice Only okay?

Vincent How's Mum?

Maurice Fine, so is everyone else.

Vincent I was only asking about Mum. (*Beat.*) You're still building it, then? Did you make an application? Dad? (*Beat.*) What if you get fined? What if they knock it down?

Maurice Then I'll build it back with these hands. That extension proves this family has a future, Vincent, I'm surprised you can't see that. (*Beat. He smiles.*) We've bored her silly, of course, with stories of you.

Vincent Who?

Maurice Irene. We all have.

Vincent Dad, I –

Maurice (*pushing through*) Esther's got a cardboard box, which I didn't know about or maybe I did, a box and a plastic bag full of your creations – clay, stuff made out of pipe-cleaners, stuff going way back. She showed Irene, spread them out. Your own little retrospective.

Vincent (*concerned*) Can we talk about Mum?

There is a noise on the stairs. Vincent looks up to see Irene making her way down. She appears to be wearing a dressing gown that matches Maurice's. Vincent stands for some reason.

Irene I expected to come down here and find you in a bloody heap, Maurice. (*To Vincent.*) We heard a noise, he thought you were burglars.

Maurice I didn't.

Irene He did. (*Beat.*) I'm Irene. (*Beat.*) Your dad showed me a photograph of you.

Vincent Oh . . . he didn't show me one of you.

Irene Sit down, please.

Irene steps into the room and walks over to the sofa. Vincent sits, but only after she's sat down.

Vincent Nice robe.

Irene Sorry?

Vincent Your dressing gowns – they match.

Irene Your dad won't admit it, but he feels the cold.

Maurice I don't.

Irene They came in a two-pack.

Vincent His and hers?

Irene Yes. (*Beat.*) Was it a good journey down?

Vincent Fine, thank you.

Irene Did you get the stopping train or the straight through?

Vincent Irene?

Irene Yes.

Vincent I'm sorry, but I don't really know anything about you.

Irene (*a little hurt*) That's okay.

Vincent I just mean I haven't been told an awful lot.

Irene Maybe if you called home once in a while . . .

Vincent I beg your pardon?

Maurice (*quickly*) Irene, why don't you –?

Irene Are you hungry? I'll make you something. Not a sandwich, though, because that'll just sit on your stomach all night. I'll find something else. Maurice?

Maurice I'm fine.

Irene stands and walks to the kitchen. She switches on the kitchen light and disappears out of sight.

Vincent (*whispered*) What are you doing wearing matching dressing gowns?

Maurice What are you talking about?

Vincent It's Monday night. You should be out there with Rowena, not in here wearing matching dressing gowns.

Maurice (*drops his voice*) I *was* out there. She's still getting over the baby, I'm not staying the night yet. And that mattress is –

Vincent She should be indoors. She should be in her old room.

Maurice Irene's got her old room. She likes it in the caravan. It isn't for ever.

Vincent (*beat; shifting forward*) I want to talk about Mum.

Maurice (*ploughing on*) What do you think of her?

Vincent Not much, if I'm honest.

Maurice Don't say that.

Vincent You're speeding up, Maurice.

Maurice I'm sorry?

Vincent You should be slowing down at your time of life and you're speeding up. It was three years between Lid and Rowena.

Maurice It's not about speeding up or slowing down. It's about needs.

Vincent Your needs?

Maurice Tell me about the course. Go on. Who are you studying? Who was your last lecture about? Throw some names at me.

Vincent I hate the course . . .

Maurice (*beat; he takes this in*) You're tired.

Vincent I'm not tired. I'm telling you how I feel. You asked me and I'm telling you I hate the fucking course.

Why aren't you looking after Mum properly? Why is there an empty bottle out there, then, on the lawn? Why isn't she your priority?

Maurice Is there something wrong with the course?

Vincent I just don't think it's me any more.

Maurice Of course it's you. It's exactly you. Listen to me. A good degree at a good university. Ivy League –

Vincent That's America.

Maurice It doesn't matter. I ache to have had that opportunity, Vincent.

Vincent *You* ache. I don't.

Irene switches out the kitchen light and enters the lounge, carrying a plate.

Irene My thoughts ran to gammon, because that's actually a good thing to eat last thing at night because it keeps the body ticking over while you sleep. It digests slowly, you see. But it looked a bit sad on the plate, just gammon, so there's salad, but you can treat that like a garnish, you don't have to eat it. Okay?

She hands Vincent the plate. Vincent takes it and gives it a withering look.

Maurice Say thank you to Irene.

Vincent (*beat; he looks at his father*) Thank you, Irene.

He puts the plate down without touching it. Irene looks hurt. She glances at Maurice.

Irene I'll leave you to it. (*Beat.*) Nice to meet you, Vincent. Esther and I changed your bedclothes, so

they should all be fresh and what have you . . .
Welcome home.

*Vincent looks up at her coldly. Irene quickly goes
upstairs, looking a little wounded. Maurice glares
at Vincent. When Irene has disappeared out of
sight, he speaks.*

Maurice (*stands*) You should go to bed, we'll talk in
the morning.

Vincent Rowena was good – I mean she was a good
fit, but this one seems –

Maurice When we lost Lydia we lost something
important. Irene is a way of replacing that.

Vincent You can't do that. We're not a football team,
Dad.

Maurice Esther needs help, Fay needs stability,
Rowena understands.

Vincent That's not how a family works, though. You
can't pick and choose –

Maurice She lost her husband and she learnt Spanish.

Vincent What are you talking about?

Maurice She didn't just sit there, she learnt Spanish.
(*Beat.*) She lent me those tapes. You remember, from
the summer? And she computerised the office, she's
loyal. You see one thing, but she's more than that and
we need her.

*Vincent looks at him strangely. Maurice hesitates
before he moves over to a plug in the corner of the
room. He switches out the Christmas lights on the*

extension. He then turns and moves for the stairs.
Vincent stands and picks up his bag.

Vincent I can't call home. I know when Mum is putting a face on things. I've had a lifetime of her telling me exactly what's on her mind and when she doesn't tell me, it's deafening. (*Beat.*) It makes me hate her . . . for letting you do this to her.

Maurice (*beat*) What did you say?

Vincent For not going when Lid did and for not putting herself first.

Maurice (*indignant*) You've thought a lot about this, have you?

Vincent Yes. I have. She's like Esther – Mum's becoming a fucking shell, just like Esther. I didn't see her emptying out. Going grey.

Maurice Don't speak about her like that. That's the way Esther is.

Vincent Not always. She's worn down. There's nothing I could do for her, but I can stop it happening to Mum.

Maurice You're tired, this is nothing coming out of your mouth. Go to bed.

Vincent No one else lives like this. (*Beat.*) Everyone I love is in this house and I can't bear to come back here.

Maurice slaps him. It's sudden and unexpected.
Vincent stands there with his bag in his hand. Both men look at each other, wondering if that really just happened. The lights fade.

93

SCENE TWO

Tuesday night. Irene is laying the table outside for dinner. She is taking real care and attention with the cutlery. Inside, Fay comes downstairs in the evening light with a magazine in her hand. She looks delicate and older than before. She wears tracksuit trousers and a sweatshirt. She makes her way to the kitchen and disappears out of view for a moment. When she emerges she has a glass of water in her hand. She moves across the lounge and heads for the garden. As she steps outside she sees Irene laying the table; she hesitates for a moment, but it's too late, Irene looks up and smiles. Fay smiles back insincerely and comes to take a seat. Fay watches her. Neither woman speaks. Fay lights up a cigarette, which noticeably perturbs Irene. Esther comes up from the bottom of the garden with a pair of gloves and some pruners in her hand.

Esther I was about to lay that.

Irene It's fine.

Esther There's a clean tablecloth –

Irene It's okay. I want more of a taverna feel for tonight.

Fay We're eating outside?

Irene It's Maurice's idea. Is there a problem?

Fay Only that it's minus two.

Irene Don't be so dramatic, Fay, it's mild. Besides, it's good for you to get an airing.

Fay gives her a look as Irene picks up a vase from her tray and places it exactly in the centre of the table. Esther and Fay watch her.

Esther (*beat*) Can I do anything?

Irene It's all under control, thank you, Esther.

Irene picks up her empty tray, smiles at the two women and heads indoors. Esther watches her go. Rowena steps out of the caravan with the monitor in her hand. She comes and takes a seat looking closely at how carefully the table has been laid.

Rowena Did you go out?

Fay When?

Rowena This afternoon.

Fay Of course not.

Rowena I didn't see you.

Fay I was in my room. I was asleep.

Rowena I thought you might have gone out? I was surprised.

Fay No surprises.

There is a slight noise from the baby monitor. Esther looks at the caravan uneasily, desperate to step over and see to the child. Rowena watches her coolly.

Esther I can go.

Rowena Leave her, she needs to work things out on her own a little bit.

Fay She's just dreaming.

Esther I wonder what about?

Rowena You crowd her, do you know that?

Esther I don't think I do.

Rowena It's not a question, you definitely crowd her. You were crowding me today, you didn't need to be there. She's my baby, Esther.

Fay She knows.

Esther I just wanted to make sure everything was . . . it was a check-up. It was important.

Rowena It was routine – and stop having mints before you pick her up.

Fay What are you talking about?

Rowena It isn't your job to worry about what your breath smells like around her, okay? I'm the one who breathes on her.

Esther Why don't you let me help you? I'm good at this.

Rowena At what?

Esther (*beat*) At bringing them up.

Rowena But she's not yours *to* bring up, Esther . . .

Pause. Fay smokes, Esther looks hard-done-by, Rowena fumes quietly.

Esther You're quite pushy now . . . when you sell on the phone. You never used to be.

Fay She's found her 'sales story' now, that's all. She's getting good at it, at last.

Esther She makes two sales a day sometimes.

Rowena And?

Esther Are you saving money?

Rowena What?

Esther Fay stops at one sale. What are you saving money for?

Rowena I don't have to answer to you.

Esther Why are you working so hard?

Rowena Stop listening to me on the phone. I made vows to Maurice not to you – you're just the babysitter.

Fay She isn't saving for anything. (*To Rowena.*) Are you? . . . *Are* you?

Rowena I'm saving for Zoë. It's good for her to have some money behind her.

Esther She's got what she needs.

Rowena I'm thinking ahead. Look at Vincent. University is expensive, isn't it?

Fay She's not even walking yet.

Rowena (*to Fay*) I said I was looking ahead. Don't you start.

Esther (*standing*) Maurice provides and we're managing fine. You don't need to save money. (*Beat.*) We're going to need another chair . . .

Esther walks quickly inside. Rowena is fuming.

Fay I always found her a blessing in disguise.

Rowena Well, I don't.

Fay She used to bring Vincent to me in the night. She'd wake me up, I'd roll over and feed him and she'd put him back to bed. I hardly moved for eighteen months.

Rowena That's terrible, Fay.

Fay It was bliss at the time. (*Beat.*) Have you ever watched her lay the table? Our domestic goddess? She does it with a ruler like a state function.

Rowena (*beat*) Maurice says we need her.

Fay Does he now?

Rowena He says she'll help us get things back to normal.

Fay And what is that exactly?

Rowena He appreciates what you're doing, Fay. Staying in. Putting the family first.

Fay You don't have to say this stuff on his behalf.

Rowena I'm saying it for me. (*Beat.*) I appreciate it.

Esther emerges from the kitchen with two chairs in her hands. She brings them outside and takes a seat. Irene follows her with a tray of starter dishes, before Maurice emerges from the kitchen with a jug of squash and some glasses. He stops at the foot of the stairs on his way out.

Maurice (*calling up*) Vincent! Tea!

Irene (*correcting him*) It's dinner.

Maurice (*calling up*) Dinner, then – come on!

Irene and Maurice follow Esther outside to the patio. Maurice puts the tray down and looks admiringly at the table.

Very nice, very European.

Everyone sits. An awkward pause around the table.

Esther Shall I call him?

Maurice I just called him, didn't you hear me?

Fay Does anyone else need a glass of wine to get through this?

Irene gives Fay a look. Pause. Everyone sits and waits. Inside the house we see Vincent come slowly down the stairs. He steps outside in silence. It's hard to judge his mood. Esther smiles and Fay watches him closely. He takes a seat.

Vincent (*beat; uncritically*) It's scented.

Fay What is?

Vincent The candle.

Maurice (*brave face*) So, Irene, talk us through this feast.

Irene It's not a feast. (*Beat.*) To start with –

Fay A starter? How many courses is this extravaganza, Irene?

Irene It's just melon and Parma ham to begin.

Maurice Lovely.

Irene Cocido for main course. (*Beat.*) It's a stew – chickpeas and chorizo.

Vincent Sounds Spanish.

Esther It is.

Vincent I understand they were your tapes. The ones Maurice borrowed over the summer?

Irene I started learning the language when Eddie passed away. I used to come home and switch them on. It felt like having someone to talk to.

Fay (*dry*) Handy, too – being able to just switch them off.

Vincent (*gently*) How long ago did he pass away, Irene?

Irene Six years. (*Beat. We glimpse an immense sadness.*) And for dessert I thought crumble, because I know Maurice is partial.

Fay (*dry*) Well, it all sounds ideal.

Maurice What a beautiful night as well.

Fay Cold.

Maurice Crisp.

Irene (*picking up a plate from the tray*) I'll play Mum, shall I?

Irene serves Maurice first. He takes the plate and reaches for the salt.

No puedo comer sal.

He puts the salt back.

Fay Meaning?

Irene 'I'm on a salt-free diet.'

Irene serves Fay next. She holds the starter dish out in front of her.

Fay (*playfully*) That's a lovely blouse, Irene. You've made a real effort.

Maurice She always dresses nicely.

Irene You're the lucky one, Fay, being able to wear jogging bottoms. I'd never get away with them. Not that I would choose to wear them, but –

Fay Thank you. I find it hard to motivate myself sometimes to make an effort.

Irene You shouldn't, you have beautiful features.

Vincent (*beat*) What's it like, working with Maurice?

Irene (*still serving the others*) I see him three times a day when he isn't on site and I can set my watch by him.

Vincent What do you actually do for my dad, Irene?

Irene I'm the office manager. (*Beat.*) He comes in to make a phone call in the morning, he writes his safety report in the afternoon and he does paperwork at three-thirty.

Fay You see more of him than we do.

Irene Occupational hazard. Living with the boss!

Maurice Irene may go part-time for a while, now she's here. (*Beat; hesitating.*) I thought we should, with Vincent home, I thought we should share our vows sooner rather than later. (*Beat.*) I want everybody here for it.

> *Fay takes this badly. Esther looks down. Rowena thinks about it for a moment.*

Fay (*to Esther*) Did you know about this?

Esther won't answer. Irene finishes serving and sits.
Everyone has food now, but no one eats. Pause.
The news is still sinking in.

Maurice A toast. (*They raise their glasses*) . . . Thank you, Irene, for this delicious meal. Thank you, Vincent, for coming home to us. The most important thing in the world is family. (*Beat.*) When it's good, and we're happy – there's no place I'd rather be than around this table.

Maurice drinks and everyone follows suit except Fay, who looks confused and hurt.

Fay Is there a date set for you two?

Irene Yes.

Fay For the registry office and for the vows here?

Maurice Just the vows. They're first, you remember that. (*Beat.*) I just want us to do it while Vincent's around. He missed Rowena's.

Rowena (*to Vincent*) We had a little toast for you.

Fay (*beat*) Excuse me.

Fay stands and walks indoors. Esther watches her go. Once inside, she disappears into the kitchen.

Irene You might not have noticed, but there are mandarin ice-cubes in the squash. (*Beat.*) It's just a mandarin segment in the middle of an ice cube. It's just summery . . .

Rowena In December?

Esther (*to Vincent*) Maurice said you were tired.

Vincent I'm fine.

Esther You should relax now you're home. Recharge the batteries for next term. I know what you're like. (*Beat.*) I'd like to know how it's all going.

Vincent hesitates, then puts his cutlery down. He takes Esther's hand.

Vincent I'm not really enjoying it, Esther.

Esther (*concerned*) Why?

Vincent I've changed my mind.

Maurice softly shakes his head. Vincent notices.

Esther About what?

Vincent The course.

Esther You're not enjoying it?

Vincent I chose it for Maurice, not for me. I realised that as soon as I got there. I'm very average at it, Esther.

Maurice You are not average.

Esther (*beat; considering*) Well . . . if you don't enjoy it . . .

Maurice gives Esther a look. Vincent squeezes her hand, gratefully.

Have you made some nice friends?

Vincent Yes. I've joined some groups. There's a nice bunch of us. I've joined a church group.

Esther smiles. It takes a moment for this to sink in for Maurice. Then, after a moment, Vincent spots his father's appalled reaction and his silence.

(*To Maurice.*) That may have come out wrong. I thought I said I'd joined a church, perhaps I said I'd killed some people.

Inside, a knock brings Fay from the kitchen over to the front door. She opens it. Jason stands and looks back at her. He has a camera bag over his shoulder.

Jason I thought you drank squash? From a jug? (*Beat.*) What are you wearing?

Fay (*defensive*) I was cold. We're eating outside.

Jason In December?

Fay Don't ask.

Jason Your blood gets thin as you get older.

Fay Turn off the charm, please, I can't cope.

Jason A tracksuit, is that a tracksuit?

Fay Is that a problem?

Jason I never saw you as a tracksuit sort of person, I suppose.

Fay Sorry to disappoint.

He looks at her for a moment, then speaks.

Jason I need to . . . (*He touches his camera.*) I'll be as quick as I can.

They stare at each other for a moment before Fay steps out of the way and lets him in. She runs her hands through her hair and straightens herself out a little. He catches her doing it; she realises and looks a bit embarrassed.

Fay Part of the job for you, is it? This sort of visit?

Jason It's called compliance. There's only so many letters we can write. We have to see if the contravention still exists.

Fay It does. (*Beat.*) I meant, couldn't they have sent someone else?

Jason I asked to come.

Fay (*beat*) Well, snap away, don't let me stop you. It's still there, you'll see it for yourself. He's added a few courses of bricks. He hasn't exactly busted a gut, but he's proven his point.

Jason Which is?

Fay It's his house, he'll do what he wants with it. (*Beat.*) You're still wearing the ring.

Jason I went through with it.

Fay Sounds like an operation. What did Debbie say about what you wrote? Your letter – splitting yourself in two?

Jason (*uneasy*) She forgave me. (*Beat.*) How's Vincent?

Vincent Back for the holidays, growing up.

Jason Lydia?

Fay (*beat*) She's gone.

Jason I'm glad.

Fay I thought you would be.

Jason It's nice to see someone putting themselves first around here. Someone other than Maurice, I mean. (*Beat.*) Do you know where she is?

Fay We stay in touch. Vincent writes to her. There's a photo of Fergus on the fridge with teeth and hair –

Jason Where have you been, Fay?

Fay I'm sorry?

Jason Where have you been? I thought you might have gone on the overland, widened your drinking circle. I went to Catford.

Fay You went to Catford to look for me?

Jason Yes, I did. You weren't in Catford.

Fay No, I wasn't. I've stayed in lately.

Jason (*dry*) Like a good wife?

Fay I'm trying. I've made a choice.

Jason It's called a sacrifice.

Fay That's what married life is all about, isn't it? You must have worked that out by now. (*Beat.*) I like the idea of you scratching around for me. Honeymoon?

Jason The Maldives.

Fay Like Tom Cruise.

Jason (*serious*) Look at you. The state of you. (*Beat.*) I've missed you.

Fay (*destabilised*) You better take your photographs. Wait here.

Fay walks away from him and emerges outside. She walks to the table.

Irene Which kind?

Vincent Of what?

Irene Religion.

Vincent It doesn't matter.

Irene Doesn't it?

Maurice Of course it matters.

Vincent It matters but it's not why I came home. (*Appealing.*) I need some advice about the course, what I should do. My tutor thinks I could make a switch early next term and still be –

Irene Are you born-again?

Vincent That's none of your business.

Maurice Irene's part of the family, therefore we'll talk about this in front of her. I have no problem with that.

Irene He doesn't have to talk about it, Maurice. It's okay. You are what you are . . .

   Maurice seethes. Vincent seems at a loss.

I went to a cathedral in Liverpool once. On a mini-break. Eddie and I. The one they say is the biggest in the country. It's twice the size of the cathedral in Sheffield, certainly. It was packed. Catholicism is alive and well in Liverpool, I thought. It's reassuring.

Maurice Why is it reassuring?

Irene If you're Catholic.

Maurice Are you?

Irene No.

Maurice So why is it reassuring?

Vincent Dad!

Irene (*defensive, and angry with Maurice*) Well, I think they're generally considered to be the good ones.

Maurice Good ones?

Irene The nice ones.

Maurice Nice?

Irene Maurice! They're generally considered to be . . . people tend to want to be Catholics . . . by and large.

Vincent (*beat*) It was probably the Metropolitan Cathedral of Christ the King.

Irene It was just a coach trip.

Maurice (*beat; to Vincent*) We've talked for hours. Proper conversations. Years of talking and this has never come up.

Vincent I've thought about things. This has never made sense to me.

Maurice You were fine all the time you were with the family, under this roof.

Vincent I don't know if I was.

Maurice When we talked about your future.

Vincent *You* talked.

Maurice *We* talked. Don't lie. When *we* talked, this never came up.

Vincent I've only been a handful of times. Don't be so small-minded.

Maurice They've got their hooks into you, though, haven't they? Why?

Vincent I need it.

Maurice People do drugs at university – my son does religion.

Jason steps outside. Maurice rises. He stares at Jason but doesn't move.

Fay (*dry*) Oh, didn't I mention . . .? The man from the council is here.

Jason (*addressing the table*) Sorry to interrupt. I just need to . . . I'll be as quick as I can.

Moving quickly, Jason starts taking photographs of the extension.

Maurice We got all your letters.

Jason You'll be given ample opportunity to state your case.

Maurice What, to you?

Jason To a magistrate, if you prefer.

Maurice (*beat*) How's your fiancée?

Jason She's my wife now.

Maurice You went through with it, then? I only hope for her sake you've stopped chasing married women.

Jason Fay isn't married to you.

Maurice Yes, she is.

Jason finishes his photographs and looks back at the table. Fay looks at him.

(*To Jason.*) Have you eaten?

Fay Maurice, don't be stupid.

Maurice (*sitting confidently*) Seriously, have a seat. Have some food. It's Spanish stew.

Vincent Dad!

Maurice Chorizo and – what was it?

Irene Chickpeas.

Rowena (*nervous*) Maurice!

Maurice Let's be civil. We can do that. I'm not what you think I am.

Jason walks down towards the patio. He looks around the table. He looks at Irene.

Jason Does she know how you do things?

Irene My name is Irene.

Jason Well, Irene, do you know how he does things?

Maurice Of course. She's chosen this family. We're very grateful.

Jason (*to Fay*) Why are you still here?

Maurice Because it's where she belongs.

Jason I was talking to Fay.

Maurice She isn't saying much back, though, is she? She's probably embarrassed. You're quite an embarrassing presence. You presume an awful lot. Have you come back for Fay, is that it? Her white knight?

Pause. Jason doesn't speak.

I didn't think so.

Jason (*beat*) If you love these women –

Maurice If . . .? You didn't expect us all to be sat here, did you? Like this? Eating three courses? We still eat together every Tuesday. We still work for each other. Vincent is an undergraduate now. Doing very well. Irene is happy to join us. It didn't really go to plan for you, did it? (*Beat.*) Sit. Be my guest . . .

Jason looks at Fay. She can't meet his gaze.

Jason Why are you still here? Please answer me that.

Fay (*with real difficulty*) I'm not as strong as Lydia.

Jason I think you are.

Without warning, he takes a photograph of her. She looks up at him, surprised.

You should see your face . . .

Jason turns and looks only at Vincent. There is a moment of connection here.

Look after your Mum, Vincent.

He takes a few steps back from the table and leaves the garden. Vincent watches him go. He walks through the house and leaves through the front door. After a moment Maurice puts down his cutlery. With difficulty, Irene reaches for the plates and starts stacking them up. Everyone is sitting in perplexed silence.

Vincent (*to Rowena*) What music did you walk down to?

Rowena What?

Vincent Before you said your vows. (*To Irene, as he hands her his plate.*) Did you know he lets you pick the music? What you walk down the stairs to? Then you write down what you want to say and so does he and then you read it and make a solemn vow. It's very simple. His own little religion. With music he lets you choose and a flower he gives you.

Maurice That's enough.

Vincent (*to Rowena*) Did he give you a flower? Esther cuts it from the garden.

Rowena 'Billie Jean'.

Vincent Michael Jackson, good choice.

Irene Do you think what your father is doing here is wrong?

Vincent It's crossed my mind.

Irene It isn't wrong. You might not understand it.

Vincent Excuse me?

Irene It isn't the worst thing in the world to love a person enough to put them first.

Fay laughs drily.

Vincent Who's he putting first?

Irene You're very young to be so angry with him.

Vincent You live with him for a while and see how you get on.

Irene (*to Vincent*) Don't talk to me like I'm your sister. I'm not Fay. I'm a fresh pair of eyes in this house, young man, and you've been using his first name so long you've forgotten who he is. This is your father.

Vincent And she's my mother, and she is, and she is, and Lydia was. Are you now as well?

Maurice How many times do I have to say we drink squash at the table, Fay?

Fay throws her wine glass across the lawn. She then hooks out the flowers from the vase in the middle

of the table and casts them onto the lawn as well.
She pours the entire bottle of wine into the empty
vase. She grips it and looks at Maurice.

Fay A fucking office manager? (*Beat. She sounds
wounded and emotional.*) I chose this family, chose
you. Chose to stay and you bring home your fucking
office manager? You must be very lonely, Irene. To
have chosen this. I hope you know what you've let
yourself in for. It's a big commitment.

Irene I've been married before.

Fay Not like this, I promise you. Not anything like
this.

Irene I know things are difficult for all of you. I'd like
to help.

Fay Why are we sitting out here and chatting in the
fucking winter? What's wrong with this family? (*Beat;
to Irene.*) I should have said you're overdressed for a
Tuesday night. There was a time when that would
have been my opener. That blouse is just the sort of
thing I would have seized on for a start . . . but the
fight's gone out of me, I think.

Maurice I know what we need, Fay. (*Beat.*) Things
will get back to normal soon.

Fay (*beat*) How can you just sit there, Esther? Are
you even listening to this? (*Beat.*) Why don't you say
something?

Esther (*strong*) We've already lost Fergus and Vincent.
I won't lose Zoë as well. If she's what it takes . . .

Vincent You haven't lost me . . .

*Esther smiles sadly and touches Vincent's face. She
turns and looks at Fay.*

Esther I made up a bed for you on the sofa when you
first came. Do you remember? There were enough
beds, but I made up the sofa for you anyway because
you asked me to. I did it properly with blankets that I
tucked under tight like a drum. (*Beat.*) Maurice spent
the night with you, and I laid upstairs. And I had to
trust him that it was the right thing to do. I trusted
him then . . . and I trust him now. (*Beat.*) Our days
used to be just him and me and work and dinner then
bed and begin again until he came home and told me
about you. Sat me down. You should have heard the
words he used, all the wonderful words to explain
you and him and me and how the three of us could
be a family and have a family. Do you really think
I shouldn't have listened? (*Sadly.*) For better or for
worse. Trust him Fay, what else is there to do . . . ?

*Esther slowly picks up her cutlery. She looks at her
plate, then at Irene.*

Don't ever speak to my son like that again.

Esther looks back at her plate. No one speaks.

Blackout.

SCENE THREE

*Wednesday night. Maurice is outside, mixing cement
and adding a course of bricks to the extension. The
garden is deserted and he is working hard.*

*Inside, Esther comes downstairs dressed in her cotton
slip and dressing gown. She is wearing make-up. She*

*steps over to the CD player and slides a CD inside.
She presses 'play'. Familiar music begins. Outside
Maurice hears it and looks up. Esther reaches down
beneath the cabinet and gets out the Scotch bottle.
She heads for the kitchen.*

*Maurice listens for a moment longer before picking
up his wheelbarrow and disappearing down the
garden for more bricks.*

*The living room is still for a moment before Fay
descends the stairs. She is dressed well, in something
approaching her old glory. She has a winter coat on
and a travel bag in her hand. She moves quickly
through the room and over to the wall where Vincent's
painting is hanging. With only a moment's hesitation
she plucks it from the wall. Esther emerges from the
kitchen with a glass of Scotch and lemonade in her
hand. Both women stop and look at one another. Fay
takes in what Esther is wearing.*

Fay It isn't your night, Esther.

Esther We swapped. Irene wanted tomorrow instead.

*Fay puts the painting down and steps over to
Esther. She looks at her sadly before throwing her
arms around her tightly. After a moment, she lets
go, picks up the painting and her bag and leaves
the house. Esther stands quietly for a moment and
looks utterly lost. The music plays.*

Blackout.

SCENE FOUR

Thursday night. Vincent walks up the garden with Zoë in his arms. He walks around the garden, singing or speaking to her very quietly before coming over to the patio. Rowena steps out of the caravan, wearing a dress. She has the phone and phone-book in her hands. She comes over to the table.

Vincent No more calls tonight.

Rowena This is the golden hour.

Vincent People are eating, you shouldn't bother them now.

Rowena People are used to it. Telesales is a way of life. Some people put me on speakerphone in the kitchen while they eat. I perform to whole families sometimes. (*Beat.*) What do you think?

Vincent (*looking down at Zoë*) She seems bunged up. Maybe it's a cold.

Rowena I meant the dress.

Vincent (*beat*) Turn around.

Rowena I'm not turning around for you.

Beat. Then she reluctantly gives him a twirl. He smiles at her and nods.

You don't think she should sleep out here, do you? Can I tell you something?

Beat. She hesitates. He looks at her.

I've got some money saved. (*Beat.*) He's great with her . . . but he's not her father . . . and what I needed

116

a few months ago is different now. I mean, I've got *her* now. (*Anxious.*) I can't tell him that, can I?

Vincent 'You made vows to me' . . . that's what he'll say.

> *Vincent sounds a little like his father. He stands, and Rowena looks at him. Inside the house, Maurice descends the stairs in a suit and a tie. During this conversation he walks over to the CD player and slides a CD in. A bottle of champagne sits on the coffee table.*

'You made vows to me. You don't remember your vows.'

Rowena (*looking down*) Not a hundred per cent.

Vincent 'You wrote them.'

Rowena I know.

Vincent 'Can't you see how that's hurtful to me?'

Rowena Stop it, that's weird. (*Beat.*) I meant them then.

Vincent He'll say that's not how marriage works.

Rowena We won't be married for much longer.

Vincent He'll say you are.

Rowena We'll be divorced soon. Now Irene's here. (*Beat; delicately.*) You know we've never . . .

> *A long beat. Rowena looks at him. Vincent gets her meaning but doesn't blink.*

Vincent He took you in. (*Beat.*) 'I'll build an extension for you with my own hands.'

Rowena I'd like to see that.

Vincent More people fall apart than stay together. What do you think that says about people?

Rowena Who's talking now?

Vincent I am.

They look at each other. She steps over to him and tucks the baby in a little.

Rowena You don't want me to stay here either, do you? (*Beat.*) Say something, then?

Vincent Come and stay with me.

Rowena (*beat*) Where?

Vincent I don't know.

Rowena (*beat*) Okay.

They look at each other again, aware of what's just happened.

Vincent We should go in.

Rowena takes the baby from him. They look at each other again and head inside.
In the living room, Maurice is sitting on the sofa with a bottle of champagne in front of him when Esther enters from the kitchen. She is wearing a pinny over a dark blue suit. Maurice can hear her behind him.

Maurice (*reaching for the champagne*) What did we drink?

Esther Asti.

Maurice (*fondly*) That's right . . . a sit-down meal for thirty-two. The King's Head pub hotel. Telegrams. Do people still send telegrams?

Esther I don't know. (*Beat.*) Shall I take that?

She walks over. He holds the bottle out to her.

Maurice I remember everything about that day. (*Beat.*) I couldn't do this without you, Esther.

Esther I think you're making a mistake with Irene.

He turns and looks at her. She takes the bottle.

I'll get some glasses.

Esther turns and heads for the kitchen. Maurice is quietly devastated by what she's said, winded almost. Rowena and Vincent enter from the garden but Maurice barely notices. She gives Vincent a look and goes straight into the kitchen with Zoë. Maurice turns and looks at his son.

Maurice (*struggling*) How do I look? All right?

Vincent nods. Pause.

So your old dad looks all right?

Vincent I've tried calling Mum, she isn't picking up.

Maurice She's never been very good with days of the week.

Vincent She isn't coming back, Dad.

Maurice (*blindly*) She'll be back.

Vincent moves to enter the kitchen when Maurice speaks and stops him.

You used to tell me when my girls were unhappy, when you were little. You always told me if I'd done something wrong. They used to think I was a mind-reader. (*Beat.*) You don't tell me any more.

Vincent You don't listen . . . Your tie is . . .

Maurice stands over by the space on the wall. He undoes his tie and starts again. He can't seem to get it the way he wants it. He turns to Vincent, appealing with the tiniest gesture for help with it. Vincent looks at him but doesn't move. Maurice goes back to wrestling with it himself.

Maurice Is the church thing to get at me?

Vincent The world doesn't revolve around you, Maurice.

Maurice We can talk about your course when this is all over. (*Beat.*) How's that?

Maurice shows him the new knot. Vincent nods.

People get married in a church, blessed in a building they never walk into again. It's the home you should say your vows in, that's where you practise them everyday.

Vincent (*reluctant*) I go to church . . . when I go, because I like the ceremony of it.

Maurice What does that mean?

Vincent I find it reassuring. The same words every week in the same order . . . the same responses.

Maurice You sound like my father. (*He taps the wall.*) Where is it? (*Beat.*) I want it back on the wall.

Vincent It's junk.

Maurice It's perfect. It's three joined-up circles like oxygen bubbles. It's you and me and your mother.

Vincent They're just circles.

Maurice You were eleven and I bought it a frame and had it dry-mounted because it's perfect. It's dry-mounted, not stuck down. Mounted like a proper painting so it could be removed and reframed without damage because that's what it is – a piece of art created by my own son. It belongs on this wall.

Irene appears at the top of the stairs. She is wearing a shimmering silver blouse and a skirt. She has a slide in her hair and is holding a single-stemmed flower in her hand. Maurice looks up at her and smiles. He reaches for the remote control and presses play. The slow snare of Ravel's Bolero starts to play from the speakers next to Vincent. Irene comes down the stairs serenely and in time to the music – she may well have practised this. Vincent watches as she comes across the carpet towards Maurice. He can't disguise his disgust. He turns and goes upstairs. Rowena enters and immediately goes after him. Disappointed, Maurice stops the music abruptly.

Maurice (*calling after him*) Vincent!

There is no reply. Maurice looks lost. Irene smiles.

Irene Will I do?

Maurice (*brave face*) Absolutely.

Maurice takes a piece of paper from his inside pocket. He starts to read.

I'm incomplete as a person . . .

Irene Are we starting right now?

Maurice Yes.

Irene Hold on. (*Beat.*) Okay.

Maurice (*reading*) I'm incomplete as a person. Pieces of me are everywhere. In the trees, in the sky, in your eyes. Pieces of me are in paintings and statues and in the books I read. If I could find all these pieces I would be whole and complete, but who could? I can only look for them. I've found one in you. One piece. It makes me more whole than I was. It fills a void. (*He turns the page.*) My father was incomplete as a person and he never once looked for a single missing piece. He was wrong not to look. (*Beat.*) For time and eternity I give myself to you. May what I am make you more whole than you are for time and eternity.

Maurice folds up his paper and tucks it back in his pocket. Irene looks at him.

Irene Mine are just bullet points . . .

She takes out a small piece of paper herself.

Thank you for the flower. Thank you for the music and letting me pick it. Eddie and I had it at our wedding, for the first dance. Torvill and Dean had just won gold and everyone was humming it . . . Eddie was my world – and when he . . . I've been searching for something. (*She comes away from the paper.*) It isn't right for someone with something to give not to have the opportunity to give it again. Love, I mean. Eddie wouldn't approve of me with just anybody, but a good man with a good heart, a gentle man who smells nice and is pleasant and loving . . . I can't see he wouldn't approve of that. I don't have sisters. I'm an only child. I'm part of something now. This house needs respect. It needs wives who act like wives not like daughters. It needs children who have respect.

I want that for you and I want to help you to get that in this house. I'll be your wife for time and eternity but I'll be a mother too and I'll make this a family again.

She folds her piece of paper.

Maurice Thank you.

Irene What you said was very nice. (*Troubled.*) You won't need anyone else now, I should have worked that in.

Maurice I need all of you.

Irene That should have been part of what I said. Can we say them again please?

The front door opens. Fay enters. Maurice rises and looks at her. She is drunk and barely holding it together. On closer inspection we realise the state she's in. Her eye make-up has run badly, her hair is a mess and she has dirty knees.

Fay 'Pieces of me are everywhere. In your eyes, in trees, in bushes, blowing around . . .'

She kicks off her high heels and drops her keys, leaving the door wide open.

'Bits of me are in paintings.' Has he covered all this yet? 'For time and eternity I'm incomplete.' (*Beat.*) Unless he's written something new, which I doubt. (*To Maurice.*) Have you written something new?

Maurice I still mean what I say.

Fay Of course you do. (*To Irene.*) Of course he does.

Fay sits down heavily on the sofa. Maurice steps over to shut the front door. Just as he does so,

Jason steps into the doorway with his car keys in his hand and wearing a black overcoat. He is holding Fay's handbag. Maurice stares at him.

Jason I brought her back.

Fay Come in, come in, of course.

Irene We haven't finished, Maurice!

Fay Don't mind us. I smell of smoke, but just push through.

Maurice You watched her get like this?

Jason No. We found her – my wife is in the car . . .

Fay Where *do* you get those awful blouses, Irene?

Jason We had a pub dinner, Debbie and I. (*He looks at Fay.*) She was in a car park, slid up between some bins with a man.

Fay Just making friends.

Maurice is horrified and ashamed. It disgusts him that Jason should be the one to find her and bring her home. He looks at him and tries to shut the door. Jason puts his hand up and stops him.

Jason Fay? What do you want me to do?

Irene Can we finish please, Maurice?

Fay Stay.

Jason and Maurice eyeball each other. Jason steps past him, moves over to Fay and stands behind her.

Don't mind us – just go for it. Heart and soul.

Maurice turns and looks at Fay. He tries to regain his composure.

Maurice (*concerned*) Where have you been, Fay?

Fay (*quietly*) Did you miss me?

Irene Maurice, please! Let's repeat our vows.

Maurice There's nothing more to say.

Irene I want to make some changes.

Fay (*drowsily*) It's too late. You've signed your life away.

Irene You be quiet.

Fay You fuck off, Number Five.

Maurice Thank you for bringing her home. You can leave us alone now. Your wife is waiting.

Fay Debbie, Debs. Pretty but not too bright.

Irene This is supposed to be my day.

Vincent comes downstairs. Jason looks at him. Fay sits up and smiles.

Fay Hello, darling.

Vincent Mum?

Vincent rushes over to Fay. He strokes away the hair from her face.

Fay Sweetheart, love, darling boy, darling baby. Don't say anything, but I think Irene's been drinking.

Vincent Mum, what's the matter? What happened to her?

Fay Jason found me in a car park making friends.

Vincent (*beat*) Mum, come upstairs.

Fay Absolutely not. Irene wants another crack at the vows and your father wants us all to be here to see it.

Vincent puts his arm round her and tries to stand her up.

Fay (*resisting*) No!

Jason Let him look after you, Fay.

Fay But I smell of cigarettes.

Vincent I don't mind.

Fay I'll have a shower, I expect.

Rowena walks downstairs, carrying the baby monitor in her hand. She walks into the room and sees Fay.

Rowena What happened?

Rowena moves over to Fay.

Fay (*beat; to Irene*) What music did you walk down to? Are you a Neil Sedaka girl? I bet you are. Lydia had 'Strawberry Fields' . . . which felt perfect.

Esther enters, carrying a tray with a champagne bottle on it and some glasses. Fay turns and looks at her fondly.

Honestly . . . she has the roughest deal. The absolute roughest. She looks after everyone and we all hate her a little bit and she hates us as well but we also love her and I think she loves us back. I hope so, Esther, I hope you do. (*Beat. She looks at Maurice.*) He's yours. He's always been yours. We just borrow him. Well, you can have him back . . .

Vincent Where was she?

Jason (*to Esther, nervously*) I found her . . . in a car park . . . My wife and I did . . .

Fay On all fours with a stranger. Between a bottle bank, and he was between me.

Irene For God's sake.

Vincent pulls Fay to him and hugs her. He looks harshly at Maurice.

Vincent (*to Jason, with difficulty*) Thank you . . . for bringing her back.

Jason She doesn't want this any more. I came to hear her say that. Fay?

Fay stays with her head buried in Vincent. Maurice walks slowly over to the sofa. He looks down at Fay being nursed by Vincent.

Maurice (*softly*) Where's the painting, Fay?

Vincent DON'T TOUCH HER. (*Beat; gently.*) It's over, Dad. It's nobody's fault. It's slipped away and that's all there is to it.

Maurice (*beat; to Jason*) He hasn't got the first idea, has he, Fay? He should come back in five years, in ten years, with that ring still on his finger. Come back and judge us then.

Maurice takes Fay's hand. He holds it, but she is barely aware. Maurice looks at Vincent, who looks back at him coldly.

You held him once, now he's holding you. Look at what we made . . . all of us. Look at this magnificent boy. (*He kisses her hand.*) Don't you miss that painting? Don't your eyes go up to the empty space on the wall every time you walk in the room? Where's the painting, Fay? (*Beat.*) Whose turn is it to cook, Esther? (*He looks up at her.*) Let's drink champagne. Vincent might paint something new. What does the rota say, Esther? Can you remember it by heart?

Esther doesn't even look at Maurice. She puts the tray down.

Esther (*with strength*) Vincent, get your mother something hot to drink. Rowena, you clear up, please. Come on, Fay.

She steps over to Fay and speaks softly to her.

Come on, I'm here.

Esther stands her up and walks her slowly to the stairs. Everyone watches as they go up together, Fay leaning heavily on Esther. They disappear out of sight.

Irene I'm having second thoughts about all this, Maurice. (*Beat.*) If Eddie was looking down, I don't know what he would be thinking. You can say what you like about church weddings, but at least no one interrupts.

Maurice looks at Jason, then at Rowena, who has her arm through Vincent's. He looks at his son for some moments before crossing the room and moving outside into the garden. He walks slowly and with difficulty through the extension, across the lawn and down to the patio. He looks at the table and then up at the caravan. He turns and looks back at the house.

Friday night. Lydia is looking around the living room.
She throws her coat over the sofa and moves closer to
the bookshelves. We hear some movement from the
kitchen. Rowena calls through.

Rowena (*off*) Lemon. Lemon and grapefruit. Cranberry,
strawberry and raspberry. (*Beat.*) Camomile, honey
and vanilla. Stop me at any point.

Lydia They all taste the same, you choose.

Rowena (*off*) I'll do a lucky dip.

Lydia takes a book off the shelf. She looks at the
back of it. She glances along the shelf and picks up
another she recognises. After a moment Rowena
comes into the room carrying a tray with five mugs
on it. She sits, with the monitor in front of her on
the coffee table. We hear a slight noise from it,
a baby's giggle. Lydia smiles and takes a seat next
to her.

Esther'll be in her element up there.

Lydia I ought to send another picture for the fridge
door. He's growing up so fast he looks different one
month to the next.

Rowena You didn't change his name, then.

Lydia Fergus stuck. (*Beat.*) I'm not sure he'll thank
me for it.

Rowena There are worse names. (*Beat.*) None spring
to mind right now, but . . .

Rowena smiles and has a sip of tea. Lydia smiles back at her. Pause.

Lydia Where is he?

Rowena On business.

Lydia (*beat*) Really?

Rowena It's what Esther said. There's a new shopping centre with completely the wrong glass in it. The wrong windows, the wrong sort. He's gone to have a look.

Lydia Tonight?

Rowena He left first thing this morning. Esther says he may quote for it, if he thinks he could do the job. It's in Salisbury. He's booked in overnight. A Travelodge.

Lydia Near a gallery?

Rowena (*she shrugs and smiles a little*) He must have known what was coming. He just didn't want to be here for it.

Lydia (*beat*) Did his office manager go with him, by any chance?

Rowena She left last night . . . I don't think she'll be back.

Lydia Fay told me all about her.

Rowena She was all right, she just wasn't us.

Lydia (*fondly*) Us? (*Beat.*) Did you say goodbye?

Rowena To Irene?

Lydia To Maurice.

Rowena doesn't answer this. She sips her tea instead.

What will you do?

Rowena (*beat*) Get the train to York. Stay in his halls for a bit. We'll take it a day at a time.

Lydia (*she takes this in*) It won't be easy with Zoë, you know, and with Vincent trying to study.

Rowena I know. (*Beat; nodding at her mug.*) Any ideas?

Lydia None.

Rowena Lemon and grapefruit. You should take the bag out or it'll be too strong.

Lydia fishes the bag from her cup with her fingers and puts it on the tray. From the monitor we hear Esther's voice. Both women listen to her talking to Fergus and Zoë for a moment.

Outside, Vincent wheels the barrow up from the bottom of the garden. He is dressed in a scruffy shirt and jeans. He stops by the extension and takes a sledgehammer from the wheelbarrow. He picks it up and begins demolishing the wall. After a few hits he bends down and starts loading the bricks into the wheelbarrow.

Inside the house Fay comes downstairs. She looks clean but tired in a pair of jeans and a shirt. She has a travel bag in her hand. Lydia stands and smiles at her.

Lydia How are we doing?

Fay Okay.

Lydia All packed?

Fay This is everything.

Fay smiles weakly and comes and sits down next to Lydia. Vincent swings the sledgehammer again and

*a larger section of the wall comes away. After a
moment Esther descends the stairs. She comes over
to sit on the sofa. Outside, Vincent loads the
barrow up with bricks.*

Esther Fergus likes it up there. He remembers it.

Fay He can't do.

Esther He does, I'm telling you. They're lying head to
toe. He's twice the size of Zoë.

Rowena He's twice as old, three times even.

Esther It's not a criticism.

Rowena (*apologetic*) Okay . . .

Esther picks up her mug and has a sip of tea.

Lydia I didn't tell you – I'm a taxpayer now.

Fay What?

Lydia I got a job.

Rowena I thought you already had a job.

Lydia A different one. My own treatment room at a
private practice. They do beauty treatments and most
things, but not Reiki – I do that for them.

Fay (*disgusted*) My God, tax. (*Beat.*) And is that full-
time?

Lydia (*dry*) You're gonna need to make more than
one sale a day, Fay, if you're going to help me with
the rent.

Fay Full-time, though . . . I feel dirty just saying it.

Lydia smiles at her and shakes her head a little.

Rowena I better take his tea to him.

Rowena stands and picks up a different mug. She heads across the room and goes outside. Vincent continues working. Rowena steps down into the extension and looks around it. Inside, Lydia and Fay catch each other's eye. They look over at Esther, who is sitting quietly.

Fay Esther? (*Beat.*) What are you thinking?

Esther (*with mixed emotions*) That it's just the two of us again.

Fay reaches for Esther's hand. The women sit in silence for a moment. There is a cry from the monitor. Esther looks up.

Lydia Leave them.

Esther One will wake the other.

Lydia They're okay.

Esther I wonder what they're dreaming about. (*Beat.*) I wonder what they'll remember. (*Beat.*) What do you think they'll even be like?

Fay They aren't anything yet, are they? That's the fun of it. The clock's ticking from now.

The three of them sit for a moment. Outside, Vincent loads up the wheelbarrow with bricks. Rowena helps him. They load it up to its tipping point. The lights fade.

The End.